SOPHIE GRIGSON
my favourite family recipes

ISBN 0 563 48886 7

Commissioning Editor: Rachel Copus
Project Editor: Catherine Johnson
Design Manager: Sarah Ponder
Designer: Diane Clouting
Typographic Styling: Paul Welti
Home Economists: Lyn Rutherford, Annie Nichols, Maxine Clark
Picture Researcher: Claire Parker
Production Controller: Kenneth McKay

Set in Helvetica Neue
Printed and bound in Great Britain by Butler and Tanner Ltd, Frome, Somerset
Jacket and laminated case printed by Lawrence-Allen Ltd, Weston-super-Mare
Colour origination by Radstock Reproductions Ltd, Midsomer Norton

Front cover photograph by Jess Koppel: *Couscous with Roast Tomatoes, Peppers and Goats' Cheese* (page 118-119)

MARKS &
SPENCER

SOPHIE GRIGSON

my favourite family recipes

contents

introduction

When Marks and Spencer asked me to put together a book of my favourite family recipes I was absolutely delighted. This gave me a chance to leaf through some of my previous books and put together a collection of some of the foods that we like to eat in our house, when we sit around the kitchen table together as a family. There are dishes for every day – *Chez Nous Shepherd's Pie*, *Chicken Stew with Parsley and Cornmeal dumpings* – as well as for high days and holidays and bigger feasts – *Crown Roast of Pork with Spiced Prune and Apricot Stuffing* or *Gratin of Courgettes with Tomatoes and Potatoes* – for when the wider family, aunts and uncles, cousins and grandparents, descend upon the house. Some of the recipes are quick to put together – just the thing for a weekday meal – whilst others require a bit of time and peace to concoct. There are recipes for those fun-time family picnics and simple mouth-watering recipes for high tea such as *Asparagus and Gruyère Quiche* or *Banana Teabread*.

It is a fact beyond dispute that your cooking has to change when you have a family. Now, I don't mean that suddenly you are going to stop cooking and eating all your favourite things, but, probably for the first time in your life, you will, sooner rather than later, have to start providing regular meals, day in day out, whether you feel like cooking or not. For me, one of the greatest pleasures of family life (I have two children) is sitting together round the supper table, enjoying something we all like to eat, and discussing this and that and the other. Our busy modern lives mean that this can't necessarily happen every single day, but I aim to make it happen several times a week, and I think we all benefit.

The result is that I have become a firm believer in the value of family recipes. I'm not talking about fancy, grand food, but nor am I heading towards the lowest common denominator. I don't like the idea of special 'children's food' at all. Sure, young mouths may not appreciate big hunks of chilli, but on the whole there is no reason why they shouldn't eat much the same food as adults, albeit in smaller proportions. Allowing them the same pleasures as us and broadening their tastes to embrace all manner of ingredients will pay handsome dividends in the long run. Oh, and the other good thing is that it saves on cooking time, and on washing up. Both big bonuses in my eyes.

Here's hoping that this book will help you to get the most out of your family meals!

Sophie Grigson

cook's notes

I adhere to certain conventions when cooking, which it may be helpful to know. All herbs used in the recipes are fresh unless otherwise stated. Always stick with following either the metric or imperial measurements for the ingredients, never a mixture of the two. All spoon measurements are rounded, unless otherwise stated. I use a 15 ml tablespoon and a 5 ml teaspoon. All eggs are large (the old size 1 or 2) and in my kitchen at least, free range. I use nothing but extra virgin olive oil for cooking and for salads, but if you find the flavour too strong, feel free to replace it with plain olive oil.

Treat timings as distinctly approximate. Remember that ovens vary, pans vary, hobs vary. All these things will affect the length of time any dish needs to cook. Judge by eye, by smell and by taste. You are the one cooking up these recipes in your own kitchen, with your own equipment, and you must be the final arbiter.

To sterilize jars, wash them in warm soapy water, then rinse in hot water. Without touching the insides, place them on a wire rack in the oven, set to 110°C/250°F/Gas Mark ¼. Leave for at least 30 minutes, until the jam is ready to be potted.

Herbs

Basil

Italy's most renowned herb, sweet, fragrant, peppery, thrilling basil, actually originated in India. However, the Italians have adopted it lock, stock, and barrel, trumpeting its starry marriage with the tomato and creating a sauce that shows it off at its most brilliant: pesto, which has now become an international megastar. I love basil but, sadly, there is basil and then there is basil and the two are not necessarily the same. Basil grown outdoors, under a mercilessly strong sun, has a peppery intensity that can set the pulse racing. Basil that has been grown under glass, in cooler climates, will look just as good, if not better, but can only compete in the tamest of ways. Most of what we can buy at home, or indeed can grow at home, will taste and smell pretty good, but doesn't reach superstar status. There's little you can do to change that, short of getting your basil flown over from Italy in the summer, and doing without in the winter.

Grow your own basil if you can, otherwise buy it in bunches or plastic packs. Avoid the 'growing basil' sold in pots in supermarkets – it rarely has any flavour at all.

Coriander Leaves

The Mediterranean countries can be split pretty neatly into those that don't and those that do. The don'ts lie, for the most part, to the north. A sighting of a leaf of coriander on the dinner plate is a rare thing indeed in Italy, France or Spain. Portugal is the exception, but then it is hardly a Mediterranean country, with its lengthy Atlantic coast. You have to travel south to northern Africa to find the truly remarkable, entrancing flavour of coriander, which grows upon you stealthily until you become quite addicted to it.

These days there is absolutely no problem buying coriander in our local shops, I'm glad to say. In fact, in supermarkets it is now the second-biggest-selling herb after parsley. Amazing when you think that only twenty or so years ago it was virtually unknown here. Try, if you can, to buy coriander from smaller Greek, Turkish, Asian or West Indian food stores, where coriander is, quite rightly, sold in beautiful big bunches for a song. Some supermarkets are now following their lead but, even so, their bunches are on the puny side in comparison. Don't stand the coriander in a glass of water on the window sill when you get home, not if you want it to last any time, that is. Pop it instead in an airtight container in the vegetable drawer of the fridge and pick it over daily, discarding any yellowing leaves.

Although there are plenty of instances where coriander is simmered into stews and sauces, I've always found this to be a total waste of time. You lose that strange and wonderful flavour that makes coriander so beguiling, and I can never detect anything much in taste terms to make up for the loss. Better to strew it on to dishes liberally at the end of the cooking time, or to process big handfuls into sauces or soups, or to toss it gleefully into salads.

Garlic

Wonderful, wonderful manna from heaven. Garlic is just essential and, what is more, it is amazingly good for you, a natural antiseptic that gives your insides a going over every time you eat it. It is practically the first thing you reach for when cooking any savoury recipe from anywhere around the Mediterranean. One of the finest (and most frequent) smells of the southern kitchen is that of garlic, and perhaps onions, sizzling in olive oil. Bliss. Olive oil and garlic… a real marriage made in heaven.

When you are buying garlic, look for heads which are firm all over, and that smell of… well, nothing very much at all. You see that garlicky smell which Britons used to be so scared of, but are now beginning to drool over just like any red-blooded Spaniard, doesn't actually exist until the moment a garlic clove is cut into or damaged in some way. As the cell walls are breached, an almost instant chemical chain reaction occurs, creating that garlicky scent and releasing it into the air. Peel a clove and you can't help but damage it a little here and there, which will release a minor whiff. That's why dishes made with torrential quantities of whole garlic cloves don't blow your head off, as long as the garlic has been cooked, which halts the process. Sliced garlic will be more pungent, but not half as smelly as chopped garlic, and a mere pale echo of crushed garlic, which has by far the strongest smell and taste of all.

Lightly browned garlic is extremely good to eat (I love the taste of golden brown garlic 'crisps', in other words slices fried in olive oil, scattered over foods), but do take care not to overdo it. Dark brown or burnt garlic is bitter and quite disgusting and it doesn't take much to ruin a whole dish. Be warned.

Oregano

Oregano is a rare thing, a herb that is actually better dried than it is fresh. There is some debate about the difference between marjoram and oregano (in fact they both share the Latin name *origanum*) but to me the main difference is that marjoram, with its warmth and sweetness, is better fresh, whilst the true delights of oregano only appear when it is dried. Custom has it, or rather had it, that oregano was the name for wild marjoram, though now commercial herb growers have muddied the issue by cultivating fresh oregano, which, may I say, is not much to write home about.

If you have a Greek or Italian deli near you, make a bee line for it and buy your dried oregano (the Greeks call it *rigani*) there for a taste of the real thing. Then you will understand why it is used with such abandon.

Rosemary

A herb that is much favoured in both Italian and French cooking. It is powerful, so needs to be used with some care, though, having said that, I think we are far too cautious with it here. The Italians have no qualms about using it with abundance, where the dish can take it, often chopping the tough leaves up very finely so that they can be eaten with ease.

When I say rosemary, I mean fresh rosemary not dried, which is quite another matter. The dried stuff is prickly, painful and horribly camphorous. Since rosemary grows easily, and is available all year round from shops, there really is no excuse for not using the fresh leaves all the time. If you do grow it, don't waste the trimmings when you cut it back – they make very good skewers for tender meats and fish, imparting their flavour from the inside out.

Sage

It is easy to think of sage as a particularly British herb, much in evidence in stuffings and sausages, but it is also a considerable favourite in Italy, where they use it with rather more panache. Here it is threaded on to skewers between chunks of meat or fish, so that its scent sinks into the flesh as they cook together; it perfumes butters for dressing pasta; and it is frizzled in hot oil to bring a new note to a tomato sauce. It goes with meat, naturally, but I think of it more in conjunction with veal than pork in Italy. Anyway, the thing is that sage is a truly glamorous herb when used well, but dried sage is an abomination. If you have any lurking on your shelves, chuck it out before you are tempted to use it. No self-respecting Italian cook would substitute dried sage for fresh – he or she would know that this musty, dusty, shrivelled shadow of its former self is not to be commended.

weekday suppers

brightside baked potatoes ■ **monster meatballs** with melting hearts ■ **prawn, sweet cicely** and tomato risotto ■ **good old hamburgers** ■ **grilled lamb chops** with tomato, olive and rosemary salsa ■ **spiced chinese spare ribs** ■ **omelette tourangelle** ■ **stir-fried noodles** with holy basil, prawns and shiitake mushrooms ■ **pork chops with marsala** ■ **fusilli with smoked trout,** rocket and basil ■ **turkey escalopes** in leek and lemon sauce ■ **gratin of cauliflower** with anchovies ■ **parsnip, carrot and cauliflower korma** ■ **potato and pepper stew** ■ **stuffed tomatoes** ■ **rosemary lamb chops** on garlicky chickpea mash with garlic jam ■ **spiced turnips and chickpeas** ■ **salmon quarter-pounders** with dill and capers

brightside baked potatoes

Emblazoned above the door to a friends' house is the word 'Brightside', a singularly incongruous name for a house with a view over vast metal air-conditioning units from the factory next door to a busy arterial road. It fits this brightly coloured dish of baked potatoes topped with spiced chicken and red peppers far better.

SERVES 4

4 BAKING POTATOES

6 TABLESPOONS NATURAL YOGHURT

SALT AND FRESHLY GROUND BLACK PEPPER

FOR THE FILLING:

2 CHICKEN BREASTS, DICED

½ TEASPOON GROUND TURMERIC

1 TEASPOON GROUND CORIANDER

1 GARLIC CLOVE, CRUSHED

1 ONION, DICED

1 TEASPOON OLIVE OIL

1 TABLESPOON SUNFLOWER OR OLIVE OIL

1 RED PEPPER, SEEDED AND DICED

4 TABLESPOONS ROUGHLY CHOPPED FRESH CORIANDER

METHOD

Pre-heat the oven to 200°C/400°F/Gas Mark 6.

Prick the skins of the potatoes all over with a fork to prevent bursting. Dampen the skins lightly, then rub with salt. Place on a baking tray and bake for about 1 hour, until tender all the way through. Season the yoghurt lightly with salt and pepper.

Meanwhile, mix the chicken with the turmeric, ground coriander, garlic, onion, olive oil and some salt and pepper and leave for 30 minutes, until the potatoes are just about cooked. Heat the sunflower or olive oil in a frying pan and sauté the chicken mixture for 2 minutes over a medium heat. Add the diced pepper and continue sautéing until the chicken is cooked through and the pepper is tender. Draw off the heat and stir in the coriander.

Cut a deep cross in the top of each potato, taking it about two-thirds of the way down towards the base. Using the thumb and index finger of both hands placed evenly between the cuts, squeeze the base of each potato firmly, until the top opens like the petals of a flower to reveal the white flesh inside. Spoon the chicken mixture into the 4 steaming potatoes, then top each one with 1½ tablespoons of yoghurt. Serve immediately.

monster meatballs
with melting hearts

These big, big meatballs have a small secret hidden away inside – a wee pool of molten cheese that oozes out as you cut into them. As long as you are careful during the initial frying (the two key tips are to make sure that the oil is good and hot and then not to fiddle around with them until they've browned underneath), they are very easy to cook. They make an excellent main course for a family supper, as people of all ages seem to love them. Serve with some sort of greenery – lightly cooked Savoy cabbage, perhaps, or a green salad – and add a generous bowlful of buttery mash, or noodles, or some baked potatoes.

SERVES 4

60 G (2 OZ) WHITE BREAD WITHOUT CRUSTS, TORN UP

500 G (1 LB 2 OZ) MINCED PORK

2 GARLIC CLOVES, CRUSHED

1 TABLESPOON FINELY CHOPPED PARSLEY

1 TABLESPOON FINELY CHOPPED MARJORAM

1 TABLESPOON FINELY CHOPPED CHIVES

A LITTLE FLOUR FOR DUSTING

30 G (1 OZ) STRONG CHEDDAR CHEESE, CUT INTO 4 CUBES

2 TABLESPOONS OLIVE OR SUNFLOWER OIL

400 G (14 OZ) TIN OF CHOPPED TOMATOES

2 TABLESPOONS TOMATO PURÉE

4 TABLESPOONS WATER

1 TEASPOON CASTER SUGAR

SALT AND FRESHLY GROUND BLACK PEPPER

METHOD

Soak the bread in cold water for about 3 minutes. Drain and squeeze out excess water firmly. Add the bread to the pork, along with the garlic, herbs, salt and pepper. Using your hands, mix and squelch it all together thoroughly to form a cohesive, mouldable mixture.

Divide the mixture into 4. Dust your hands with flour. Take the first portion of meatball mixture and roll it into a ball. Use your finger to hollow out a hole leading right to the centre of the ball. Insert a cube of Cheddar and then use your fingers and hands to close up the hole securely. Repeat with the remaining meatball mixture and cheese. If you have time, chill the meatballs for 30 minutes or so before cooking.

Heat the oil in a heavy-based frying pan over a fairly high heat. Add the meatballs, then let them sit, without moving, for 2–3 minutes, until they roll over easily if you shake the pan gently. Repeat until nicely browned all over. Pour in the tomatoes and all the remaining ingredients. Stir around the meatballs and bring up to the boil. Reduce the heat to a quiet simmer, then cover the pan with a lid, and leave to cook gently for about 30 minutes, turning the meatballs carefully once in a while. If the sauce still seems a bit watery, remove the lid and boil down for a few minutes longer. Taste and adjust the seasoning, then serve.

prawn, sweet cicely
and tomato risotto

This has to be one of the most heavenly risottos of all. I'm partial to a seafood risotto at the best of times, but this one, made with big juicy prawns and the subtle aniseed softness of sweet cicely, is very special indeed. If you really can't lay your hands on any sweet cicely, then try it with chervil instead.

It is absolutely crucial that you use raw prawns (it doesn't matter so much if they have been frozen, as long as they have thawed before use) and they must be in their shells. Head-on prawns are even better than headless ones. The shells are used to transform the stock into a shellfish stock, thus perfuming the rice right to the very core. Tiger or king prawns are just the ticket. You will not need any extra Parmesan for serving – too much will overwhelm the flavour of the prawns and sweet cicely.

SERVES 4-6

550 G (1 LB 4 OZ) HEAD-ON RAW PRAWNS IN THEIR SHELLS
   OR 500 G (1 LB 2 OZ) HEADLESS RAW PRAWNS IN THEIR SHELLS
85 G (3 OZ) UNSALTED BUTTER
1.2 LITRES (2 PINTS) FISH, VEGETABLE OR CHICKEN STOCK
2 SHALLOTS, CHOPPED
2 GARLIC CLOVES, CHOPPED
300 G (10 OZ) RISOTTO RICE, E.G. VIALONE NANO, ARBORIO OR CARNAROLI
1 SMALL SPRIG OF ROSEMARY (ABOUT 4 CM/1½ IN LONG)
1 BAY LEAF
250 G (9 OZ) RIPE TOMATOES, SKINNED, SEEDED AND CHOPPED
2 TABLESPOONS CHOPPED PARSLEY
1 GENEROUS GLASS OF DRY WHITE WINE (AROUND 200 ML/7 FL OZ)
3 TABLESPOONS CHOPPED SWEET CICELY
30 G (1 OZ) FRESHLY GRATED PARMESAN CHEESE
SALT AND FRESHLY GROUND BLACK PEPPER

METHOD

Peel the prawns and reserve the flesh. Heat about 15 g (½ oz) of the butter in a pan large enough to take the stock with plenty of room to spare. When foaming, add the prawn shells and heads and stir about until they turn a pretty shellfish pink. Now pour in the stock and 600 ml (1 pint) of water and bring up to the boil. Simmer for 30 minutes to draw the flavour out of the prawns. Strain the shells out of the stock when it is done.

Meanwhile, return to the prawns. If you can see a black line running down their backs, make a little slit with the tip of a sharp knife down the back, then remove the fine black gut that lies just below the surface. If they are tiger or king prawns, or other large prawns, chop each one in half or thirds.

Now down to business. Bring the stock back up to boiling point if necessary, then turn the heat down under the pan to a mere thread, so that the stock stays hot but does not boil away. Melt 45 g (1½ oz) of the remaining butter in a wide pan. Fry the shallots and garlic very gently in the butter until translucent, without browning. Now add the rice, rosemary and bay leaf to the pan and stir about for around 1 minute, until the rice becomes translucent. Scrape in the tomatoes and parsley and pour in the wine. Season with salt and plenty of pepper, then bring up to a bare simmer. Stir continuously until all the liquid has been absorbed. Now add a generous ladleful of stock and keep stirring until that has all been absorbed. Repeat this process until the rice is just the right side of *al dente* – i.e. tender but with a slight firmness to it, though definitely not chalky. The consistency should be verging on soupy, as it still has a couple of minutes to go. The time taken for the liquid to be absorbed and the rice to be cooked should be about 20–25 minutes.

Stir in the prawns and sweet cicely and cook, stirring, for another 2–3 minutes, until the prawns have turned pink. Stir in the remaining butter and the Parmesan. Taste and adjust the seasoning, then serve.

good old hamburgers

When they are made properly, with good minced beef – try asking your butcher to mince some chuck steak or even sirloin steak for you – home-made hamburgers are a great pleasure. I usually grill them, but you could tart them up no end by frying them, then deglazing the pan with a slug of wine, reducing and finishing with some cream and a little mustard to make a luxurious sauce. Whether you grill or fry, test them for doneness in exactly the same way as you would a steak.

SERVES 4

675 G (1 LB 8 OZ) LEAN MINCED BEEF
½ ONION, GRATED OR VERY FINELY CHOPPED
½ TABLESPOON WORCESTERSHIRE SAUCE
1 TABLESPOON VERY FINELY CHOPPED PARSLEY
LEAVES FROM 2 SPRIGS OF THYME, FINELY CHOPPED
1 EGG, LIGHTLY BEATEN (OPTIONAL)
OIL, OR A COMBINATION OF OIL AND BUTTER, FOR GRILLING OR FRYING
SALT AND FRESHLY GROUND BLACK PEPPER

TO SERVE:
4 BUNS, SPLIT OPEN AND LIGHTLY TOASTED ON THE INSIDE
SHREDDED LETTUCE LEAVES
SLICED TOMATO
DILL-PICKLED CUCUMBERS, SLICED
TOMATO KETCHUP, MAYONNAISE,
    TABASCO, OR YOUR FAVOURITE RELISH

METHOD

Mix the beef with the onion, Worcestershire sauce, parsley, thyme, and salt and pepper. Use your fingers to squelch it all together thoroughly. If the mixture seems rather crumbly, add a little beaten egg to hold it together. Divide into 4 and shape into nice round patties about 2 cm (¾ in) thick, then grill or fry.

To grill, brush each burger with a little oil and grill close to a thoroughly pre-heated grill until browned and crusty on the outside, but still moist and tender on the inside.

To fry, heat a little oil or oil and butter in a frying pan and fry the burgers over a high heat until nicely browned outside and done to your taste on the inside.

Sandwich in the buns together with lettuce, tomato and pickled cucumber, salt and pepper, and whatever sauces or relishes you happen to like best.

grilled lamb chops with tomato, olive and rosemary salsa

Serving a salsa, a fresh-tasting sauce made of finely chopped raw ingredients, with grilled lamb chops is a very modern way of upgrading them into something rather stylish. Though you can warm the salsa through gently if you prefer, I rather like the combination of sizzling hot meat with a cool salsa. It also means less last-minute fiddling and one less pan to wash up!

SERVES 4

4 LAMB CHOPS
A LITTLE OIL

FOR THE SALSA:
225 G (8 OZ) WELL-FLAVOURED TOMATOES, SKINNED,
   SEEDED AND FINELY DICED
5 PIECES OF SUN-DRIED TOMATO, CHOPPED
8 BLACK OLIVES, PITTED AND ROUGHLY CHOPPED
1 SHALLOT, FINELY CHOPPED
1 GARLIC CLOVE, CRUSHED
1 TEASPOON FINELY CHOPPED ROSEMARY LEAVES
A GENEROUS PINCH OF SUGAR
½ TABLESPOON BALSAMIC OR SHERRY VINEGAR
3 TABLESPOONS EXTRA VIRGIN OLIVE OIL
SALT AND FRESHLY GROUND BLACK PEPPER

METHOD

Make the salsa at least an hour before eating. Mix together all the ingredients except the salt. Cover loosely and leave at room temperature (or in the fridge if it is for more than 4 hours). Taste and adjust the seasoning, adding a little salt if needed. Serve either at room temperature or warm gently in a small pan.

Brush the chops lightly with oil and grill fairly close to the pre-heated grill until crusty and brown, turning once. Season with salt and pepper and serve with the salsa.

spiced chinese spare ribs

I love sticky, grilled spare ribs. You can't possibly eat them tidily and neatly, and half the fun would be lost if you tried. The only refinement to introduce to the table is plentiful fingerbowls. I prefer to grill the ribs in groups of 3 or 4 – easier to handle than large sheets, but not as fiddly as individual ribs – and I always blanch them first to ensure that the meat stays meltingly tender. Although they are nicest grilled (particularly over an outdoor barbecue, in which case I'd suggest you double the quantities as there's nothing like fresh air to sharpen the appetite), they can also be roasted in the oven if it makes life easier.

SERVES 4 AS A FIRST COURSE

1.5 KG (3 LB) PORK SPARE RIBS

FOR THE MARINADE:

1 HEAPED TEASPOON SZECHUAN PEPPERCORNS OR BLACK PEPPERCORNS

7 TABLESPOONS HOISIN SAUCE

1½ TABLESPOONS CLEAR HONEY

3 GARLIC CLOVES, CRUSHED

2 TABLESPOONS RICE WINE OR DRY SHERRY

1 TABLESPOON CHINESE BLACK VINEGAR OR RED WINE VINEGAR

METHOD

Divide the sheets of spare ribs into small clumps of 3 or 4 ribs, for easy handling. Blanch them in boiling water for 30 minutes.

Dry-fry the peppercorns (either sort) over a high heat until they start to smell aromatic. Cool them and grind to a powder. Mix with the remaining marinade ingredients and slather thickly over the spare ribs. Set aside for at least 1 hour, preferably 3–4 hours, or even overnight in the fridge.

To cook the ribs, pre-heat the grill (or barbecue) thoroughly. Grill them fairly slowly, about 15 cm (6 in) away from the heat, turning frequently, until they are crisp and catching at the edges. This should take a good 15 minutes, so if necessary, move the ribs further away from the heat so that they don't get burnt to a crisp.

If you prefer, you can cook them in the oven, pre-heated to 220°C/425°F/Gas Mark 7. Place the ribs on a wire rack over a roasting tin and roast for 20–25 minutes until crisp and slightly frazzled.

omelette tourangelle

A big fluffy omelette flavoured with *fines herbes*, filled with soft goats' cheese and served with a roast tomato sauce. If you can't get chervil, then substitute a small amount of dill weed, fennel leaves or sweet cicely.

SERVES 2 GENEROUSLY

5 EGGS

3 TABLESPOONS CHOPPED *FINES HERBES*
(A MIXTURE OF TARRAGON, PARSLEY, CHERVIL AND CHIVES)

A GENEROUS KNOB OF BUTTER

60 G (2 OZ) YOUNG SOFT GOATS' CHEESE OR CRUMBLED, DERINDED, SEMI-SOFT GOATS' CHEESE

SALT AND FRESHLY GROUND BLACK PEPPER

FOR THE ROAST TOMATO SAUCE:

8 PLUM TOMATOES, HALVED

3 WHOLE GARLIC CLOVES (UNPEELED)

1 SPRIG OF THYME

1 SPRIG OF ROSEMARY

½ TEASPOON CASTER SUGAR

2 TABLESPOONS OLIVE OIL

METHOD

Pre-heat the oven to 200°C/400°F/Gas Mark 6.

To make the sauce, place the halved tomatoes cut-side up in an oiled, shallow ovenproof dish in a single layer. Tuck the garlic cloves, thyme and rosemary among them. Sprinkle with the sugar, season with salt and pepper and drizzle over the olive oil. Place in the oven and roast uncovered for 40–50 minutes, until the tomatoes are patched with brown. Remove the thyme and rosemary twigs, then tip the entire contents of the dish into a food processor. Process until fairly smooth, then sieve. Taste and adjust the seasoning, and reheat when needed.

Beat the eggs energetically with some salt and pepper, then stir in the herbs. Heat half the butter in a wide frying pan until it foams. Add half the eggs and make an omelette in the usual way. When it is just about cooked through, but still slightly damp and runny on top, dot half the cheese down the middle. Flip the sides over to cover and slide it out of the pan on to a warm plate. Repeat with the remaining eggs and cheese. Serve the omelettes with the roast tomato sauce.

stir-fried noodles with holy basil, prawns and shiitake mushrooms

I have a passion for stir-fried noodles spiced up with the vivid flavours of South-east Asia. I play around with all kinds of extra ingredients, but this is a combination, with the scent of barely wilted holy basil, the sweetness of prawns and the meaty texture of shiitake mushrooms, that I particularly love. If you can get fresh egg oil noodles, you will find that they are absolutely perfect for stir-frying, with a delicious slippery texture. As with all stir-frying, prepare and gather all the ingredients around you, combining the ones that go into the wok together in one bowl, before you start cooking. The going is too fast to have to rush off in search of some missing ingredient in mid-session.

SERVES 3-4

450 G (1 LB) FRESH EGG OIL NOODLES (FROM CHINESE SUPERMARKETS)
    OR 250 G (9 OZ) DRIED EGG THREAD NOODLES (FROM MOST
    ORDINARY SUPERMARKETS)

4 TABLESPOONS GROUNDNUT, VEGETABLE OR SUNFLOWER OIL,
    PLUS A LITTLE EXTRA IF USING DRIED NOODLES

3 GARLIC CLOVES, CHOPPED

2.5 CM (1 IN) FRESH ROOT GINGER, FINELY CHOPPED

½ RED ONION, FINELY CHOPPED

1-2 RED CHILLIES, SEEDED AND FINELY CHOPPED

115 G (4 OZ) SHIITAKE MUSHROOMS, STEMS DISCARDED, THICKLY SLICED
    (OR BUTTON MUSHROOMS IF YOU CAN'T FIND SHIITAKE)

115 G (4 OZ) SHELLED RAW PRAWNS, ROUGHLY CUT UP IF LARGE

A GOOD HANDFUL OF HOLY OR ORDINARY BASIL LEAVES
    (ABOUT 30-40 G/1⅓ OZ)

4 SPRING ONIONS, FINELY CHOPPED

2 TABLESPOONS FISH SAUCE

2 TEASPOONS SESAME OIL

½ TABLESPOON CASTER SUGAR

JUICE OF 1 LIME

TO SERVE:

3 TABLESPOONS (ABOUT 40 G/1½ OZ) ROASTED PEANUTS, FINELY CHOPPED

FISH SAUCE

CHOPPED RED CHILLI OR CHILLI SAUCE

LIME WEDGES

METHOD

If using dried noodles, cook as directed on the packet. Drain thoroughly and, if not using immediately, toss with about ½ tablespoon of oil.

    Put a roomy wok over the heat and leave until hazy. Now add the oil, leave for a few seconds to heat through, then add the garlic, ginger, onion and chilli. Stir-fry for 30 seconds or so, then add the mushrooms. Stir-fry for 2-3 minutes, until beginning to soften. Next throw in the prawns and stir-fry until they are just pink. And now the noodles go in, and will need a minute or two of stir-frying to mix with all the other ingredients. Set aside a few of the basil leaves to garnish the dish, then add the rest to the pan with all the remaining ingredients. Stir-fry for a matter of 1–2 minutes, just long enough to wilt the basil but not to kill its peppery fragrance, and to mix everything nicely.

Turn out into bowls and scatter the finely chopped peanuts and reserved basil leaves over the top. Serve immediately, with extra fish sauce on the table, as well as chopped chilli or chilli sauce and lime wedges for those who want them.

pork chops with marsala

A recipe for a quick supper with a touch of class. The sweetness of the Marsala reduces down to a lovely sauce.

SERVES 4
4 PORK CHOPS
2 TABLESPOONS OLIVE OIL
1 SPRIG OF ROSEMARY
200 ML (7 FL OZ) MEDIUM-SWEET MARSALA
4 STRIPS OF LEMON ZEST
1 TABLESPOON LEMON JUICE
SALT AND FRESHLY GROUND BLACK PEPPER

METHOD

Pat the chops dry with kitchen paper, then brown slowly on both sides in the olive oil in a frying pan that the chops fit into snugly. Pour off the excess fat, turn the heat down and add all the remaining ingredients. Simmer, half-covered, for 20 minutes, turning the chops once. Discard the lemon zest and rosemary. Remove the chops from the pan and keep warm. Boil the juices remaining in the pan until they are reduced to a thin layer on the base. Taste and adjust the seasoning, pour over the chops and serve.

fusilli with smoked trout,
rocket and basil

This dish takes just minutes to make – the rocket, basil and smoked fish cooking instantly in the heat of the pasta.

SERVES 4

A BIG HANDFUL OF ROCKET LEAVES

400 G (14 OZ) FUSILLI OR OTHER PASTA SHAPES

6 TABLESPOONS EXTRA VIRGIN OLIVE OIL

JUICE OF ½ LEMON

2 GARLIC CLOVES, CRUSHED

12 LARGE BASIL LEAVES, SHREDDED

175 G (6 OZ) SLICED SMOKED TROUT, CUT INTO SHORT THIN STRIPS

SALT AND FRESHLY GROUND BLACK PEPPER

METHOD

If the rocket leaves are fairly large, tear them up roughly. If they are tiny, 5 cm (2 in) or so in length, tear or snip them in half. Prepare all the remaining ingredients.

Cook the fusilli in a large pan of lightly salted water until just *al dente*. Drain well and return to the pan, set over a low heat. Toss in the olive oil, lemon juice, garlic, a little salt and plenty of pepper. Stir for a couple of seconds, then add the rocket and basil and toss again to mix evenly. Draw off the heat and finally toss in the trout. Serve immediately.

turkey escalopes in leek and lemon sauce

Turkey escalopes or turkey breast steaks take no time at all to cook (far quicker than, say, a whole chicken breast) and, as long as they are not overdone, are a most useful basis for a mid-week supper. They do need a sauce with a bit of oomph, though, since more often than not they are almost as light on taste as they are in colour. Here they are served with leeks and lemon, and scattered with a few chives just before serving.

SERVES 4

4 TURKEY ESCALOPES
30 G (1 OZ) BUTTER
1 TABLESPOON SUNFLOWER OIL
2 LEEKS, WHITE PART ONLY, CUT INTO MATCHSTICKS
1½ TABLESPOONS FLOUR
300 ML (½ PINT) MILK
½ TABLESPOON DIJON MUSTARD
FINELY GRATED ZEST AND JUICE OF ½ LEMON
FRESHLY GRATED NUTMEG
SALT AND FRESHLY GROUND BLACK PEPPER
CHOPPED CHIVES, TO GARNISH

METHOD

Season the escalopes with salt and pepper. Heat the butter and oil in a wide frying pan. When foaming, add the escalopes and fry for about 3–4 minutes on each side, until lightly browned and just cooked through. If necessary, cook them in two batches. Remove from the pan and set aside.

Add the leeks to the pan and stir until they begin to wilt. Now sprinkle over the flour and stir for about 30 seconds. Gradually whisk in the milk, bringing the sauce to the boil and simmering for about 5 minutes, stirring occasionally, until the sauce is thick and smooth.

Stir in the mustard, lemon zest, salt, pepper and nutmeg and return the escalopes to the pan, nestling them down into the sauce and overlapping slightly if necessary. Simmer for about 2 minutes, long enough to heat the turkey through thoroughly. Draw the pan off the heat and add enough of the lemon juice to sharpen the sauce without making it overwhelmingly acidic. Serve at once, scattered with chives.

gratin of cauliflower
with anchovies

Cauliflower has a special affinity with anchovies and here, both as fillets and as essence, the anchovies come into play to upgrade cauliflower cheese to a much more stylish dish than usual, more than good enough to eat all on its own.

SERVES 4

1 SMALL CAULIFLOWER, TRIMMED AND BROKEN INTO FLORETS
    (ABOUT 375 G/13 OZ PREPARED WEIGHT)

4 TABLESPOONS FINE BREADCRUMBS

2 TABLESPOONS VERY FINELY CHOPPED PARSLEY

2 TABLESPOONS FRESHLY GRATED PARMESAN CHEESE

6 CANNED ANCHOVY FILLETS, HALVED LENGTHWAYS

15 G (½ OZ) BUTTER

FOR THE SAUCE:

1 SMALL SHALLOT, CHOPPED

2 TABLESPOONS OIL FROM THE CAN OF ANCHOVIES, OR OLIVE OIL

30 G (1 OZ) PLAIN FLOUR

450 ML (16 FL OZ) MILK

1½ TABLESPOONS FRESHLY GRATED PARMESAN CHEESE

1-2 TEASPOONS ANCHOVY ESSENCE OR SAUCE

SALT AND FRESHLY GROUND BLACK PEPPER

METHOD

Pre-heat the oven to 200°C/400°F/Gas Mark 6.

Cook the cauliflower florets in salted, boiling water until just *al dente*. Take great care not to overcook the cauliflower to a grey grimness. Drain thoroughly and place in a greased, shallow baking dish, in as even a layer as you can manage.

To make the sauce, cook the shallot gently in the oil, until tender. Sprinkle over the flour and stir in. Cook for a minute, stirring, then draw the pan off the heat and gradually mix in the milk, a little at a time. Bring to the boil, then reduce the heat and leave to simmer very gently for 5–10 minutes, until the sauce is good and thick. Stir in the Parmesan and anchovy essence or purée. Season with pepper, then taste and add salt if needed.

Pour the sauce evenly over the cauliflower. Mix the breadcrumbs, parsley and Parmesan and sprinkle evenly over the surface. Arrange the anchovy fillets in a lattice pattern over the surface and then dot with butter. Bake for 25–30 minutes, until browned and sizzling. Serve immediately.

parsnip, carrot and cauliflower korma

This is a mild but warmly spiced curry, thickened with yoghurt and ground almonds. Serve with rice and relishes, such as mango chutney and sour lime pickles. You can adapt this curry to practically any vegetables that you have to hand, as long as you add those that take less time to cook, 5–10 minutes or so after the slow-cooking root vegetables.

SERVES 4

300 G (10 OZ) PARSNIPS

350 G (12 OZ) CARROTS

1 MEDIUM ONION, FINELY CHOPPED

4 TABLESPOONS SUNFLOWER OIL

1 TABLESPOON GROUND CUMIN

2 TEASPOONS GROUND CORIANDER

1 TEASPOON GROUND CINNAMON

1 TEASPOON GROUND TURMERIC

2 GARLIC CLOVES, FINELY CHOPPED

2.5 CM (1 IN) FRESH ROOT GINGER, VERY FINELY CHOPPED

1 GREEN CHILLI, SEEDED AND VERY FINELY CHOPPED

300 ML (½ PINT) GREEK-STYLE YOGHURT

45 G (1½ OZ) GROUND ALMONDS

300 G (10 OZ) SMALL CAULIFLOWER FLORETS

SALT

FINELY CHOPPED FRESH CORIANDER OR PARSLEY, TO GARNISH

METHOD

Cut the parsnips and carrots into 1 cm (½ in) slices or, if they are large, cube them.

In a pan large enough to take all the ingredients, fry the onion in the oil until golden brown. Stir in all the dry spices and, when well mixed, add the garlic, ginger and chilli. Stir gently for 1 minute. Stir in the yoghurt, a tablespoon at a time, then add the almonds. Cook, stirring, for 2 minutes.

Stir in 300 ml (½ pint) of water and some salt, then add the parsnips, carrots and cauliflower. Cover and simmer gently for 20–25 minutes, until the vegetables are almost done, stirring occasionally. Uncover the pan and simmer for 5 minutes or so. Taste and adjust the seasoning. Sprinkle with fresh coriander or parsley before serving.

potato and pepper stew

This makes a perfect supper dish, as long as you can get good chorizo to enliven the mixture of potatoes and peppers.

SERVES 4

1.25 KG (2 LB 12 OZ) POTATOES

3 TABLESPOONS OLIVE OIL

115 G (4 OZ) COOKING CHORIZO, SKINNED AND ROUGHLY SLICED

1 RED PEPPER, SEEDED AND DICED

1 GREEN PEPPER, SEEDED AND DICED

2 GARLIC CLOVES, CRUSHED

½ TEASPOON SPANISH PAPRIKA (PIMENTÓN)

1 BAY LEAF

SALT AND FRESHLY GROUND BLACK PEPPER

METHOD

Peel the potatoes and cut into roughly 2.5 cm (1 in) chunks.

Warm the oil over a moderate heat in an earthenware *cazuela* or a wide, heavy frying pan. Add the chorizo and fry briskly until lightly browned. It will fall to pieces, but this doesn't matter. Reduce the heat and add all the remaining ingredients. Pour over just enough water to cover. Bring to the boil and simmer, stirring occasionally, for 20–30 minutes, until the potatoes are cooked and the liquid has reduced by about half. Taste and adjust the seasoning. Serve with plenty of good bread to mop up the juices.

stuffed tomatoes

The stuffing is a classic Sicilian mixture of flavours: currants and pine nuts, here with the sharpness of capers and the saltiness of black olives. Try and choose tomatoes that are a deep, ripe red as they will have more flavour.

SERVES 4

4 MEDIUM TOMATOES

½ TABLESPOON OLIVE OIL

FOR THE STUFFING:

1 SMALL RED ONION, FINELY CHOPPED

2 GARLIC CLOVES, FINELY CHOPPED

2-3 TABLESPOONS OLIVE OIL

45 G (1½ OZ) STALE FINE BREADCRUMBS

30 G (1 OZ) PITTED BLACK OLIVES,
   FINELY CHOPPED

1 TABLESPOON CAPERS, DRAINED AND
   FINELY CHOPPED

1½ TABLESPOONS CURRANTS

1 TABLESPOON PINE NUTS

2 TABLESPOONS CHOPPED PARSLEY

SALT AND FRESHLY GROUND BLACK PEPPER

METHOD

Cut the tops off the tomatoes and scoop out the flesh (save the tops and flesh for making the sauce). Season the insides with a little salt and leave upside down on a wire rack to drain for 30 minutes or so, while you make the stuffing.

Pre-heat the oven to 200°C/400°F/Gas Mark 6. Place the onion, garlic and 2 tablespoons of olive oil in a frying pan and cook over a medium heat until the onion is tender. Add the breadcrumbs, raise the heat slightly and fry until golden (add a little extra oil if necessary). Scoop into a bowl and mix with all the remaining stuffing ingredients.

Pack the stuffing into the tomatoes and snuggle them together in an oiled ovenproof dish. Drizzle over the remaining ½ tablespoon of olive oil and bake for 15 minutes until nicely browned.

rosemary lamb chops on garlicky chickpea mash with garlic jam

Chickpea mash has become a very trendy accompaniment of late, and it is easy to see why. It is cheap to make, especially if you use dried chickpeas, and very easy too, as long as you remember to soak the chickpeas overnight. The finished tawny mash can be made gorgeously garlicky, with a slight lick of lemon in it to take the edge off the leguminous quality of chickpeas. It goes especially well with lamb, and then to finish the combination off with a flourish there's a surprisingly delicious garlic jam.

If you have any mash left over, it reheats well, and is rather good served with shavings of Parmesan and a knob of butter as a starter.

SERVES 4

4 SMALL LAMB CHOPS
LEAVES OF 1 SMALL SPRIG OF ROSEMARY
A LITTLE OLIVE OIL
SALT AND FRESHLY GROUND BLACK PEPPER

FOR THE MASH:
225 G (8 OZ) DRIED CHICKPEAS, SOAKED OVERNIGHT
3 TABLESPOONS OLIVE OIL
JUICE OF ½ LEMON

FOR THE GARLIC JAM:
1 LARGE HEAD OF GARLIC
60 G (2 OZ) GRANULATED OR CASTER SUGAR
125 ML (4 FL OZ) WATER
1 SMALL SPRIG OF ROSEMARY
1 DRIED RED CHILLI

METHOD

Take the head of garlic for the garlic jam and separate into individual cloves. Peel the whole lot of them. Cut 1 clove into long, thin needles for the chops. Slice 3 of them for the mash and leave the rest whole for the jam.

Make slits in the lamb chops and push in the slivers of garlic and the rosemary leaves. Season with pepper only. Cover and set aside until needed.

For the mash, drain the chickpeas and put into a pan with enough water to cover generously. Do not add any salt. Bring up to the boil, boil hard for 5 minutes, then reduce the heat and simmer gently until tender – this will take 1–2 hours, depending on the age and size of the chickpeas. Drain the chickpeas, reserving about 300 ml (½ pint) of their cooking liquid. Place them in a food processor with the sliced garlic, olive oil, salt and pepper and the juice of ½ a lemon. Process to a mash, gradually drizzling in enough of the cooking water to give a smooth but soft purée that is almost, but not quite, runny – you may not need all the reserved liquid. Taste and adjust the seasoning, adding more lemon juice if needed. Transfer to a pan and warm through gently, if necessary, while the lamb chops are cooking.

While the chickpeas are simmering, make the garlic jam. Drop the whole garlic cloves into a small pan of boiling water, bring back to the boil, simmer for 2 minutes, then drain. Put the sugar, water, rosemary and chilli in a saucepan and stir over a low heat until the sugar has completely dissolved.

Now add the blanched garlic and simmer gently for about 40 minutes until the cloves are completely tender. Tip into a small bowl with the cooking syrup and leave to cool.

Pre-heat the grill thoroughly. Brush the lamb chops lightly with oil and grill close to the heat for about 3 minutes on each side. Season with salt. Divide the mash between 4 warmed plates and lay a lamb chop on top of each. Spoon some of the garlic jam on to each plate and serve.

spiced turnips and chickpeas

This is adapted from a Moroccan recipe for a tangine of lamb, turnips and chickpeas. I've jettisoned the lamb but kept the original blend of aromatic spices and the honey sweetener. It is still substantial enough to work as a main course, served over a bed of couscous or rice.

SERVES 4

175 G (6 OZ) DRIED CHICKPEAS, SOAKED OVERNIGHT

675 G (1½ LB) MEDIUM TURNIPS, PEELED IF NECESSARY AND CUT INTO 1 CM (½ IN) CUBES

30 G (1 OZ) UNSALTED BUTTER

1 TABLESPOON SUNFLOWER OIL

1 ONION, COARSELY GRATED

1 TEASPOON GROUND CINNAMON

1 TEASPOON GROUND GINGER

1 TEASPOON GROUND CUMIN

½ TABLESPOON GROUND CORIANDER

1 TABLESPOON CLEAR HONEY

2 TABLESPOONS CHOPPED FRESH CORIANDER

SALT AND FRESHLY GROUND BLACK PEPPER

METHOD

Drain the chickpeas and cook in unsalted water until almost, but not quite tender. This can take anything from 1 hour to a staggering 3 hours. Drain, reserving the cooking water. Blanch the turnips for 2 minutes in boiling water, then drain.

Heat the butter and oil in a wide pan and add the chickpeas, onion, turnips, ground spices and enough of the reserved chickpea water to just cover. Cover and simmer for 15 minutes.

Stir in the honey, half the chopped coriander, salt and plenty of pepper. Simmer, uncovered, for 10–15 minutes or until the liquid is reduced to a thick sauce. Sprinkle with the remaining chopped coriander and serve.

salmon quarter-pounders
with dill and capers

These salmon burgers are a great hit with children and adults alike, and an excellent way of introducing fish to the wary. Serve them with deliciously crisp shoestring chips and proper coleslaw.

SERVES 4

450 G (1 LB) SKINNED SALMON FILLET, VERY FINELY DICED
   (ABOUT 3 MM/⅛ IN CUBES)
2-3 TABLESPOONS CHOPPED DILL, FENNEL OR CHIVES
45 G (1½ OZ) SHALLOT, GRATED OR VERY FINELY CHOPPED
1½-2 TABLESPOONS SMALL CAPERS, ROUGHLY CHOPPED
1½ TABLESPOONS MAYONNAISE
A GOOD SQUEEZE OF LEMON JUICE
SALT AND FRESHLY GROUND BLACK PEPPER

TO SERVE:
4 CIABATTA ROLLS OR OTHER GOOD-QUALITY ROLLS, HALVED
MAYONNAISE
2-3 CRISP LETTUCE LEAVES, FINELY SHREDDED
MANGO CHUTNEY
2 TOMATOES, SLICED
LEMON WEDGES

METHOD

Mix together all the ingredients for the burgers, then chill the mixture for at least 30 minutes to firm it up. Divide into 4 portions and form each portion into a 'burger' about 1 cm (½ in) thick. Keep cool until needed.

Prepare all the accompaniments. Pre-heat the grill thoroughly. Line the grill rack with foil. Grill the burgers and the bread rolls about 5–7.5 cm (2–3 in) away from the heat. Allow about 4–5 minutes for the burgers and don't turn them over – they'll cook through anyway, and the more you handle them the more likely they are to collapse before they are fully cooked. Once they are done, they will be a little sturdier. You will, of course, need to turn the halved rolls over to toast both sides.

Spread a little mayonnaise on the base of each roll, then top with shredded lettuce. Lay a salmon quarter-pounder on top, smear over a little mango chutney, then top with a few slices of tomato. Spread a little mayonnaise on the cut side of the roll tops and clamp them on firmly. Press down with the heel of your hand, then dish up, with lemon wedges on the side, and eat.

2 family get-togethers

stir-fried prawns with honey and spices ■ **salt cod croquettes** ■ **filo cigars** filled with crab and coriander ■ **grilled köfte** ■ **sage, anchovy** and tomato fritters ■ **salmon and sorrel parcels** ■ **sweet potato fritters** ■ **caesar salad** ■ **nuoc mam gung** ■ **barbecued corn on the cob** with olive and lemon butter ■ latin american **bean soup** ■ **thai beef salad** ■ **glazed gammon** ■ **grilled sardines** with warm red pepper and fennel vinaigrette ■ **rocket and spiced salmon salad** with honey, lime and chilli dressing ■ **tabbouleh**

stir-fried prawns
with honey and spices

This is a marvellous treat of a first course or light main course for a special occasion. I can see that you might have doubts. I quite agree that honey and prawns don't sound too promising together, but, believe me, in this instance it is a combination that works. The honey plays a relatively quiet, but not unimportant, role tempered by the saltiness of soy sauce, garlic and spices. This is definitely not breakfast with prawns on top.

For a starter, serve the prawns just as they are, with some good bread to mop up the juices. For a main course, serve them with rice and maybe some stir-fried mangetout or broccoli.

SERVES 4

16 LARGE, RAW PRAWNS IN THEIR SHELLS (TIGER PRAWNS OR KING PRAWNS)

1½ TABLESPOONS SUNFLOWER OIL

FOR THE MARINADE:

2 GENEROUS TABLESPOONS HONEY

4 TABLESPOONS DRY SHERRY

2 TABLESPOONS DARK SOY SAUCE

½ TEASPOON CHINESE FIVE-SPICE POWDER

2 GARLIC CLOVES, FINELY CHOPPED

2.5 CM (1 IN) FRESH ROOT GINGER, GRATED

METHOD

Mix together the marinade ingredients and pour them over the prawns. Turn to coat evenly, then cover and marinate for at least an hour, or longer, in which case be sure to put them in the fridge. Bring back to room temperature before cooking. Turn the prawns once in a while as they marinate.

Take the prawns out of the marinade. Heat a wok or a wide frying pan over a high heat until it smokes and then add the oil. Give it a couple of seconds, then add the prawns and stir-fry for about 1 minute, until they have all turned pink. Pour in the marinade and 2 tablespoons of water. Let the liquids bubble down until they are well reduced and syrupy, stirring constantly – a matter of a few minutes – and serve immediately.

Don't forget to pass round plenty of napkins for all those sticky fingers.

salt cod croquettes

When they are freshly cooked, with a generous proportion of salt cod to potato, these croquettes are absolutely irresistible. If you've tried them in Portugal, and rejected them as far too stodgy and salty, then I suggest you try making your own. You'll soon notice the difference.

Buy salt cod from a good Portuguese or Indian Deli. To prepare salt cod, cover with cold water and leave for 24–36 hours, changing the water at least 3 times (preferably 4–5) to remove excess salt. Drain well before using.

MAKES 16–18

225 G (8 OZ) SALT COD, SOAKED AND DRAINED

350 G (12 OZ) FLOURY POTATOES, BOILED IN THEIR SKINS

1 SMALL ONION, FINELY CHOPPED

2 GARLIC CLOVES, FINELY CHOPPED

2 TABLESPOONS FINELY CHOPPED PARSLEY

1–2 EGGS, LIGHTLY BEATEN

SUNFLOWER OR OLIVE OIL, FOR DEEP-FRYING

SALT AND FRESHLY GROUND BLACK PEPPER

METHOD

Place the salt cod in a wide pan and cover with water. Bring slowly to a quiet simmer, and simmer for 5–10 minutes, depending on thickness, until it flakes easily. Drain, and flake with your fingers, discarding the skin and bones. Using a fork and your fingers, tear the fish into fine threads.

Peel the potatoes and mash thoroughly or pass through the fine blade of a *mouli-legume* – the latter is probably the better method.

Mix the cod and potatoes with the onion, garlic, parsley, pepper and salt if needed. Add enough egg to form a cohesive stiff mass – at this stage use your hands to mix and work the paste. Let it cool completely.

Take egg-sized pieces of the mixture and, using 2 tablespoons, shape them into small rugby-ball croquettes. Deep-fry a few at a time in hot oil at 180°C/350°F/ Gas Mark 4 until richly browned. Drain briefly on kitchen paper and eat straight away.

If you want to reheat any, pop them back in hot oil for a few minutes to crisp up.

filo cigars filled with crab and coriander

Here the crisp filo pastry encloses a blissfully oozy filling of crab, coriander and cream cheese. Shaped like a cigar, this is probably the easiest of ways to use filo pastry. Serve as a first course, allowing three or four cigars per person (add a little mixed green salad to the plates), or just as something to savour with drinks. Use fresh crabmeat, not frozen, which isn't worth its price. One fairly large dressed crab will contain about the right amount.

MAKES ABOUT 18

225 G (8 OZ) MIXED WHITE AND BROWN CRABMEAT

115 G (4 OZ) CREAM CHEESE

1 TABLESPOON CHOPPED CORIANDER

1 TABLESPOON CHOPPED PARSLEY

1 TABLESPOON LEMON JUICE

6–10 SHEETS OF FILO PASTRY, DEPENDING ON SIZE

60 G (2 OZ) UNSALTED BUTTER, MELTED

SALT AND FRESHLY GROUND BLACK PEPPER

METHOD

Flake the large pieces of white crabmeat, if necessary. Beat the cream cheese with the herbs, lemon juice, salt and pepper. Mix in all the crabmeat.

Cut each sheet of filo pastry into long strips about 13–15 cm (5–6 in) wide. Cover with a sheet of greaseproof paper and cover that with a tea-towel wrung out in cold water.

Pre-heat the oven to 200°C/400°F/Gas Mark 6. One at a time, take a strip of filo, brush with melted butter and place a teaspoon of the crab mixture at one end, shaping it into a neat sausage but leaving a good 2 cm (¾ in) border. Roll the strip of filo up to form a neat cylinder, flipping over the edges as you go, to prevent the filling from falling out. Place on a greased baking sheet. Repeat until filling and filo are all used up. Brush the cigars with any remaining butter. Chill until needed.

Bake for 10 minutes, until golden brown. Eat as soon as they've cooled enough not to burn your mouth.

grilled köfte

Istanbul's Sultanahmet *Köfte* Shop, near the Blue Mosque, is reckoned to serve the best *köfte* (minced meat 'balls') in town. People of all classes crowd into the shop at lunchtime to down a quick plate of the famous *köfte*. On the walls there are framed poems proclaiming their glory.

The ingredients are disarmingly few – minced beef, bread, onion, salt and pepper. The secret, they say, lies in the quality of the meat. Prime cuts from cattle raised in different areas of the country are used. Every morning the different batches of meat are blended carefully to get just the right balance!

You can order a side salad of lettuce, tomato, cucumber and feta cheese, or of plain white beans; you can tart up your *köfte* with a spoonful of yoghurt, or a sprinkling of chilli flakes and oregano, but other than that the formula is set.

SERVES 4

2 THICK SLICES OF DAY-OLD WHITE BREAD, CRUSTS REMOVED

450 G (1 LB) BEST-QUALITY MINCED BEEF OR LAMB

1 ONION, GRATED OR VERY FINELY CHOPPED

1 TEASPOON GROUND CUMIN

OLIVE OIL

SALT AND FRESHLY GROUND BLACK PEPPER

TO SERVE:

CHILLI FLAKES

DRIED OREGANO

METHOD

Soak the bread in water for 10 minutes. Drain and squeeze dry, then crumble. Mix with the meat, onion, cumin, salt and pepper, then whizz in a processor or pass through a mincer. Knead the mixture with your hands for a few minutes until smooth and cohesive. Divide into 12 portions and roll each one into either a tubby sausage shape or a small rugby ball. Brush with oil and grill for 5–6 minutes, until just cooked through but still slightly pink at the heart. Serve with chilli and oregano for those who want to spice them up. A salad of tomato, lettuce and cucumber is a good accompaniment.

sage, anchovy and tomato fritters

This recipe, with its deep-fried morsels cherished in a crisp batter, is delightfully dual-purpose. Serve the fritters alone, sprinkled with a little salt and a squeeze of lemon juice, as a warm pre-prandial bite with drinks before you get down to the main business of the meal. Or, turn them into a starter by piling them onto a mound of watercress dressed with balsamic vinegar and extra virgin olive oil.

There's far more batter than you will need, but it is such a lovely, light, crisp one that I was loath to change the balance of ingredients to reduce quantities. I'm afraid that it won't keep, but if you are prepared to carry on frying, and have extra stocks of sage, tomato and anchovies, you might make your way through a fair amount of it.

SERVES 6 WITH DRINKS

OLIVE OIL AND/OR SUNFLOWER OIL,
  FOR DEEP-FRYING
12 CANNED ANCHOVY FILLETS
18 SAGE LEAVES
2 PLUM TOMATOES, SKINNED, SEEDED
  AND CUT INTO LONG STRIPS
SALT
LEMON WEDGES, TO SERVE

FOR THE BATTER:
225 G (8 OZ) PLAIN FLOUR, SIFTED
½ TEASPOON SALT
1 EGG, SEPARATED
1 TABLESPOON SUNFLOWER OIL
300 ML (½ PINT) LAGER
125 ML (4 FL OZ) COLD WATER

METHOD

To make the batter, sift the flour with the salt. Make a well in the centre and add the egg yolk, oil and half the lager. Mix, gradually drawing in the flour to make a smooth batter and adding more lager as you go until it is all incorporated. Whisk in the water. Let the batter stand for 30 minutes if you have time. Immediately before using, whisk the egg white until it forms soft peaks and then fold it into the batter.

Use a proper deep-fryer, or fill a deep frying pan with a 2 cm (¾ in) depth of oil, or half fill a wok. For something like this I usually use a half-and-half mixture of olive and sunflower oil. Heat it up until there is a gentle heat haze – about 180°C/350°F/ Gas Mark 4, or until a cube of bread fizzles instantly as soon as it enters the oil and begins to brown within 20 seconds. Dry the anchovies, wiping off the oil with kitchen paper (otherwise the batter tends to float off them). One by one, dip the sage leaves, anchovies and strips of tomato into the batter, coating completely, then slide them into the hot oil. Deep-fry until puffed and golden brown, turning once. Drain quickly on kitchen paper and sprinkle the sage and tomato fritters with a little salt. Serve immediately, with the lemon wedges.

salmon and sorrel parcels

The earthiness and richness of salmon are blessed by the acidity of sorrel. Make a quick sorrel sauce to go with grilled or baked salmon, but if you have a little more time, try these parcels of salmon and sorrel wrapped in pastry. Get the upper portion of salmon, if possible, as it will be thicker and chunkier.

SERVES 4

450 G (1 LB) SALMON FILLET, CUT INTO 4 PORTIONS

60 G (2 OZ) SORREL

1 EGG YOLK

350 G (12 OZ) SHORTCRUST PASTRY (SEE PAGE 141)

45 G (1½ OZ) BUTTER, SOFTENED

SALT AND FRESHLY GROUND BLACK PEPPER

METHOD

Season the salmon with salt and pepper. Shred the sorrel finely. Beat the egg yolk with a tablespoon of water.

Divide the pastry into 4 and roll each piece out thinly into a rectangle. Smear a quarter of the butter over the centre of each rectangle, covering a square roughly the same size as the salmon portion. Pile a quarter of the sorrel over the butter and lay a portion of salmon, cut-side down, on the sorrel. Wrap up neatly, to form a parcel, trimming off excess pastry and pressing the edges together to seal. Set the parcels on a greased baking tray, turning them the right way up, with the joins neatly tucked away underneath. If you wish, cut little shapes out of the trimmings of the pastry – leaves, fish or whatever – and arrange them artfully on each parcel, gluing them in place with a little of the egg-yolk glaze. Leave to rest in the fridge for 30 minutes (or longer, if necessary). Pre-heat the oven to 220°C/425°F/Gas Mark 7.

Brush the parcels generously with the egg-yolk glaze and bake for about 20 minutes.

sweet potato fritters

Lime, sweet potato and chilli are a magic combination, the vibrant flavours of lime and chilli preventing the rich sweet potato from being overwhelming. Together they make a great first course.

SERVES 6-8

3 SWEET POTATOES, PREFERABLY ORANGE-FLESHED

85 G (3 OZ) PLAIN FLOUR

1 TEASPOON GROUND CORIANDER

2 EGGS, LIGHTLY BEATEN

SUNFLOWER OIL, FOR DEEP-FRYING

SALT AND FRESHLY GROUND BLACK PEPPER

TO SERVE:

4 SPRING ONIONS, FINELY CHOPPED

1–2 FRESH RED CHILLIES, SEEDED AND FINELY SHREDDED OR CHOPPED

1 LIME, CUT INTO WEDGES

METHOD

Boil the sweet potatoes in salted water until barely tender. Drain and leave until cool enough to handle. Do not peel. Slice into discs about 5 mm (¼ in) thick. Season the flour generously with salt, pepper and the ground coriander, then spread out on a plate. Pour the eggs into a shallow bowl or plate.

Heat the oil to 180°C/350°F/Gas Mark 4. One by one, using a fork, dip the sweet potato slices into the flour and then into the beaten egg, and then back into the flour to coat them evenly. At each stage, make sure they are completely coated – excess is better than parsimony here. Fry in small batches until golden brown for about 5 minutes, turning occasionally. Drain briefly on kitchen paper. Serve hot, scattered with spring onions and chillies and with a wedge of lime to squeeze over.

caesar salad

There are many recipes for this most famous of salads, invented in the 1920s by Caesar Cardini at his restaurant in Tijuana, Mexico. The original didn't include anchovies, but they often creep in nonetheless. The final preparation (which I've simplified a little) can be done discreetly in the kitchen, or more dramatically at the dinner table. If you choose to perform publicly, make sure you have a very large bowl so that you don't shower your audience with lettuce.

SERVES 6

2 COS LETTUCES

3 SLICES OF STALE WHITE BREAD, CRUSTS REMOVED,
   CUT INTO 1 CM (½ IN) CUBES

3 GARLIC CLOVES

150 ML (¼ PINT) EXTRA VIRGIN OLIVE OIL

2 EGGS

½ CAN OF ANCHOVY FILLETS, FINELY CHOPPED
   OR ½ TEASPOON WORCESTERSHIRE SAUCE

JUICE OF 1 LEMON

30 G (1 OZ) FRESHLY GRATED PARMESAN CHEESE

SALT AND FRESHLY GROUND BLACK PEPPER

METHOD

In advance: Wash the lettuces and dry well. Store in the fridge in a plastic bag until needed. Fry the cubes of bread with the garlic in 5 tablespoons of the olive oil, until golden and crisp. Drain the croûtons on kitchen paper. Put the eggs into a pan, cover with water and bring to the boil. Boil for 1 minute, then drain and run under the cold tap.

At the last minute: Tear the lettuce leaves into manageable pieces and place in a large salad bowl. Pour over 6 tablespoons of olive oil and toss to coat each leaf. Add the anchovies or Worcestershire sauce, croûtons, lemon juice, pepper and a little salt. Toss. Finally, break in the eggs, taking care not to get specks of shell into the salad, and scatter with the Parmesan. Toss or turn again to mix evenly. Now, with all the work done, you can serve the salad.

nuoc mam gung

Simple as a recipe can be, this Vietnamese dipping sauce is a real joy if you have even the most minimal liking for the flavours of the Far East. It's gingery, sweet, hot, sharp and salty all at once. Try serving it with plainly grilled prawns or chicken. Once you've had a taste, you will probably come up with a hundred and one other ways to use it.

The recipe comes from *The Simple Art of Vietnamese Cooking* by Binh Duong and Marcia Kiesel (Simon & Schuster).

MAKES ABOUT 125 ML (4 FL OZ)

5 CM (2 IN) FRESH ROOT GINGER, FINELY CHOPPED

2 TABLESPOONS CASTER SUGAR

2 SMALL FIERY FRESH RED CHILLIES, CHOPPED

2 GARLIC CLOVES, CHOPPED

½ SMALL LIME, PEELED AND SECTIONED

2 TABLESPOONS FISH SAUCE

METHOD

Pound the ginger, sugar, chillies and garlic in a mortar with a pestle to form a syrupy sauce. Add the lime sections and pound again, working them into the mixture. Finally, work in the fish sauce. Serve at room temperature, with rice or as a dipping sauce. The sauce can be kept, in an airtight jar, for up to a week in the fridge.

barbecued corn on the cob
with olive and lemon butter

Barbecued fresh sweetcorn on the cob, streaked with brown, is juicy and tender and has a superb, sweet-smoky taste, emphasized by the saltiness of olives in the flavoured butter as it melts over the hot kernels. Soaking the corn plumps up the kernels, ensuring that they don't dry out over the hot charcoal. This is *my* version of barbecued corn.

Alternatively, you could cook them in the husk. This method produces a less smoky, more purely sweetcorn flavour. If you choose to leave the husks on, the cobs will still need to be soaked in water for a good 30 minutes. Shake off excess water, then grill over a moderate heat for about 15 minutes, turning frequently.

SERVES 6

6 HEADS OF CORN ON THE COB
SUNFLOWER OIL

FOR THE BUTTER:
60 G (2 OZ) BLACK OLIVES, PITTED
115 G (4 OZ) UNSALTED BUTTER, SOFTENED
FINELY GRATED ZEST OF ½ LEMON
1-2 TABLESPOONS LEMON JUICE
1 SMALL GARLIC CLOVE, CRUSHED

METHOD

Either place all the ingredients for the butter in a food processor and whizz until smooth, or chop the olives very, very finely and mash with the butter and remaining ingredients. Taste and add extra lemon juice if needed. Pile into a bowl, cover loosely and chill.

Strip the husks and silky threads off the corn. Immerse in a bucket of lightly salted water and leave to soak for at least 30 minutes and up to 3 hours. Just before barbecuing, pat dry, brush with oil, then cook over a moderate heat, turning, until patched with brown on all sides. Eat the hot corn with the chilled butter.

latin american bean soup

This soup is based on the wonderful bean soups of Latin America, with the elements stolen from one country and another. Melded together they create what is, paradoxically, my idea of the perfect cold-weather, winter comfort food, filling and richly flavoured with a flurry of fresh garnishes that lift it from mere starchy warmth into a joy of a dish.

Sometimes I flavour the soup with tomato but I love it, too, made with coconut milk, which blends gently with the soft beans. The results are different but both are very good. The soup can be made a day in advance and tastes all the better for being reheated. The quantities below make a filling main course for six or a less substantial but still sturdy first course for 8–10, which could simply be followed with good bread, a salad and some well chosen cheese, or cured meats and sausages.

SERVES 8-10

500 G (1 LB 2 OZ) PINTO BEANS, OR MIXED DRIED BEANS

115 G (4 OZ) PANCETTA, BACON OR LARDONS, DICED

2 ONIONS, CHOPPED

2 LARGE CARROTS, DICED

2 CELERY STICKS, DICED

4 GARLIC CLOVES, CHOPPED

3 TABLESPOONS SUNFLOWER OR VEGETABLE OIL

1 HEAPED TABLESPOON CUMIN SEEDS

1 TABLESPOON DRIED OREGANO

EITHER 2 X 400 G (14 OZ) TINS OF CHOPPED TOMATOES OR
   600 ML (1 PINT) COCONUT MILK

4 TABLESPOONS DRY SHERRY

JUICE OF 1 LIME

SALT AND FRESHLY GROUND BLACK PEPPER

FOR THE BOUQUET GARNI:

3 SPRIGS OF PARLSEY

2 SPRIGS OF SAVORY OR THYME

2 BAY LEAVES

1 SMALL SPRIG OF ROSEMARY

TO SERVE:

150 ML (¼ PINT) SOURED CREAM OR CRÈME FRAÎCHE

1 AVOCADO, PEELED, STONED AND DICED AT THE LAST MINUTE

6 SPRING ONIONS, THINLY SLICED

2 RED CHILLIES, SEEDED AND VERY FINELY CHOPPED

SMALL BUNCH OF CORIANDER, ROUGHLY CHOPPED

2 LIMES, CUT INTO WEDGES

Tie the bouquet garni together with string. Soak the beans for 4 hours, then drain thoroughly. Sweat the pancetta, onions, carrots, celery, garlic and bouquet garni in the oil over a low heat for 10–15 minutes. Now add the beans and enough water to cover by about 7.5 cm (3 in). Bring up to the boil and boil hard for 10 minutes, reduce the heat and simmer gently, covered, until the beans are very tender – around 1–2 hours.

Now add the cumin, oregano, tomatoes or coconut milk, sherry, lime juice, salt and pepper. Simmer for another 30 minutes, stirring occasionally with a wooden spoon and crushing some of the beans against the side of the pan, until you have a thick soup, studded with whole beans. Remove the bouquet garni. Taste and adjust the seasoning (starchy beans appreciate plenty of salt).

Reheat the soup thoroughly when ready to serve, adding a splash of water if it seems overly thick. Put all the serving bits and bobs into small bowls and arrange them in the centre of the table. Ladle the hot soup into bowls and pass around, encouraging people to help themselves from the selection of garnishes in the bowls.

thai beef salad

I ate very little beef when I was in Thailand. The sight of butcher's stalls in markets, open to the sun and awash with flies, was enough to put anyone off eating most meat in fact. However, I pushed that to the back of my mind when it came to this salad. Back here, where you can be sure of getting high-quality, tender steak, I think it tastes even better than it did on its home patch. Raw vegetables are added to contrast with the meat and the spice of the dressing. I've chosen tomato and cool cucumber, although others, such as sweet peppers or carrots, could be used instead. The beef and the dressing can be prepared in advance, but don't put the salad together until the very last minute.

SERVES 6 AS A STARTER, 4 AS A MAIN COURSE

450-675 G (1-1½ LB) HIGH-QUALITY LEAN STEAK, SUCH AS FILLET,
   RUMP OR SIRLOIN
OIL, FOR GRILLING OR FRYING
3 TABLESPOONS FRESHLY SQUEEZED LIME JUICE
3 TABLESPOONS FISH SAUCE
1 TABLESPOON SUGAR
4 SHALLOTS, THINLY SLICED
2 GARLIC CLOVES, CRUSHED
2 SMALL THIN RED CHILLIES, SEEDED AND THINLY SLICED
6-8 LETTUCE LEAVES
CHOPPED CORIANDER
CHOPPED CHIVES
½ CUCUMBER, PEELED AND SLICED 5 MM (¼ IN) THICK
2 TOMATOES, CUT INTO EIGHTHS

METHOD

The meat can either be grilled or roasted.

To grill: heat the grill until hot, then brush the steak with oil and grill close to the heat until browned on the outside, but still rare inside.

To roast: pre-heat the oven to 240°C/475°F/Gas Mark 9. Heat a little oil in a flameproof dish until it is very hot. Add the meat and brown it quickly over a fierce heat. Transfer to the oven and roast for 10–15 minutes.

Whichever method you use, err, if anything, on the side of undercooking rather than overcooking the beef as it will continue to cook a little in its own heat as it rests. Leave to cool for at least 5 minutes, then slice thinly.

Mix together the lime juice, fish sauce and sugar, stirring to dissolve the sugar. Add the shallots, garlic and chillies. Make a bed of lettuce on a serving dish and pile the beef in the centre. Spoon over the dressing and scatter with coriander and chives. Arrange the cucumber and tomato around the edge.

glazed gammon

A large joint of glazed gammon looks pretty impressive and, as long as you allow plenty of time, it is very easy to cook. It will need to be soaked first, then boiled (well, simmered really), and then gets a final spell in the oven to gloss the glaze.

SERVES 8-10

1 GAMMON JOINT, WEIGHING AROUND 2.7 KG (6 LB)

1 ONION

1 CARROT

1 BAY LEAF

A FEW SPRIGS OF PARSLEY

FOR THE GLAZE:

2 TABLESPOONS DIJON OR ENGLISH MUSTARD

2 TABLESPOONS DEMERARA SUGAR

WHOLE CLOVES, TO DECORATE

METHOD

Soak the gammon joint overnight in cold water, then drain well. If you don't have time to do this, you can accelerate the process by putting the joint into a pan of cold water, bringing it to the boil and letting it simmer for 5 minutes. Then throw out the water, which will take a fair amount of salt with it.

Put the soaked or blanched joint into a large pan with the onion, carrot, bay leaf and parsley. Cover with cold water and bring slowly to the boil. Cover and simmer lazily for 2 hours, topping up the water level regularly with more hot water. Leave the joint to cool for 30 minutes in its cooking liquid if you plan to serve it hot, or longer at your convenience if you wish to serve it cold.

Lift the joint out of the liquid on to a board and wipe it dry. Carefully peel off the skin: start by making a couple of cuts just through the skin itself, not the fat underneath, so that you can get a hold of it, then pull it off, without removing the fat. While you are at it, taste the stock. If it isn't too salty, save it for making soup – it's especially good for a dried pea soup.

Pre-heat the oven to 220°C/425°F/Gas Mark 7.

Transfer the joint to a roasting tin. Smear the fat with the mustard, then press the sugar firmly and evenly all over it. Using the tip of a sharp knife, score the fat with parallel lines, first in one direction, then at an angle, to form diamonds. Finally, press a clove into the centre of each diamond. Roast the joint for about 25 minutes until nicely browned and glazed.

If you are serving the joint hot, let it rest for 20 minutes before carving. Otherwise, leave it to cool slowly in its own time.

grilled sardines with warm red pepper and fennel vinaigrette

An easy dish for an easy summer barbecue, when sardines are plump and fresh, peppers ripe and plentiful and the fennel is tall and handsome. And if the rain buckets down, as it so often does, move everything back indoors and heat up that grill.

SERVES 4

8-12 SARDINES, DEPENDING ON SIZE, SCALED AND CLEANED

8-12 SMALL SPRIGS OF FENNEL

A LITTLE OLIVE OIL

COARSE SALT

FOR THE VINAIGRETTE:

1½ TABLESPOONS GOOD-QUALITY RED WINE VINEGAR

1 TEASPOON DIJON MUSTARD

5 TABLESPOONS OLIVE OIL

3 TABLESPOONS CHOPPED FENNEL

1 SMALL RED PEPPER, GRILLED, SKINNED, SEEDED AND FINELY DICED

SALT AND LOTS OF FRESHLY GROUND BLACK PEPPER

METHOD

Pre-heat the grill or get the barbecue going well in advance. Rinse the sardines and pat dry. Tuck a sprig of fennel in the stomach cavity of each fish. Either grill or barbecue the fish brushed lightly with oil, seasoning with coarse sea salt as you turn, until just cooked through – 3–5 minutes on each side, depending on the size of the fish and the strength of the heat.

Meanwhile, whisk the vinegar with the mustard, salt and loads of pepper in a small saucepan. Whisk in the olive oil, then stir in the fennel and red pepper. Heat through without boiling.

Lay the sardines on plates and spoon over some of the vinaigrette. Serve immediately.

rocket and spiced salmon salad
with honey, lime and chilli dressing

This recipe is a good example of how to use rocket as a sturdy but harmonizing support for other ingredients with a strong presence. It serves as a cushion for wedges of salmon, coated in crushed spices and then fried. Together the rocket and salmon make an excellent, quickly prepared first course, or even the main course of a light meal.

SERVES 6 AS A STARTER, 4 AS A MAIN COURSE

450 G (1 LB) SKINNED SALMON FILLET

1½ HEAPED TABLESPOONS FREEZE-DRIED GREEN PEPPERCORNS

1½ HEAPED TABLESPOONS CORIANDER SEEDS

OLIVE OIL

115 G (4 OZ) ROCKET LEAVES

4 PIECES OF SUN-DRIED TOMATO IN OLIVE OIL, CUT INTO LONG THIN STRIPS

FOR THE DRESSING:

2 TABLESPOONS CLEAR HONEY

JUICE OF 1 LIME

1-2 TEASPOONS CHILLI SAUCE

1 TABLESPOON SESAME OIL

1 TABLESPOON FISH SAUCE

2 TABLESPOONS WATER

METHOD

To make the dressing, put all the ingredients into a small pan and stir over a low heat, without letting them boil, until smoothly mixed. Leave to cool.

Cut the salmon into 4–6 portions, depending on how many people you are feeding. Crush the green peppercorns and coriander coarsely in a mortar, then spread out on a plate. Brush the salmon pieces lightly with olive oil on both sides, then coat in the crushed peppercorns and coriander. Heat about 1 tablespoon of oil in a wide frying pan over a high heat. Fry the salmon pieces for 1–2 minutes on each side, until cooked to your liking (I think it best slightly underdone and translucent in the centre, but not everyone agrees).

As the fish cooks, quickly toss the rocket with enough of the dressing to coat it nicely, then arrange on individual plates. Lay the salmon on the salad, scatter over the sun-dried tomato strips, then drizzle a little more dressing over the salmon. Serve straight away.

tabbouleh

This Moroccan salad is a wonderfully fresh, zingy mixture of couscous (it is usually made with leftover couscous but it's worth preparing a batch from scratch) with oodles of chopped fresh herbs and lots of lemon juice. It is a perfect summer salad, lovely as part of a mixed buffet (and handy, since the flavours improve on keeping for 24 hours) or, indeed, just as a side dish with cold chicken or grilled prawns, or good cheese and pitta bread. For a more Middle Eastern feel, serve with warm pitta bread, hummus, spiced black olives and taramasalata.

SERVES 6

140 G (5 OZ) QUICK COUSCOUS OR 310 G (11 OZ) COOKED COUSCOUS

6 TABLESPOONS FINELY CHOPPED PARSLEY

3 TABLESPOONS CHOPPED MINT

3 TOMATOES, SKINNED, SEEDED AND VERY FINELY DICED

½ RED ONION, VERY FINELY CHOPPED

JUICE OF 1½-2 LEMONS

4 TABLESPOONS OLIVE OIL

SALT AND FRESHLY GROUND BLACK PEPPER

METHOD

Pour 300 ml (½ pint) of boiling water over the couscous and leave for 20 minutes, stirring once or twice, until all the water has been absorbed.

Mix with all the remaining ingredients. Taste and adjust the seasonings. Cover and leave overnight.

Stir and taste again. Serve at room temperature.

3 weekend lunches

chicken stew with parsley and cornmeal dumplings ▪ **daube of beef** with cannellini beans and rosemary ▪ **lancashire hotpot** ▪ **crown roast of pork** with spiced prune and apricot stuffing ▪ **roast rack of lamb** with a herb crust ▪ **moussaka** ▪ **pan-fried venison** with port and orange sauce ▪ **chez nous shepherd's pie** ▪ **cauliflower** and tomato crumble ▪ **chicken with tarragon** ▪ **porc aux pruneaux de tours** ▪ **roast cod** with a coriander crust ▪ **laksa lemak** ▪ **chicken** with jerusalem artichoke stuffing ▪ **monkfish** with garlic and rosemary ▪ **pilaff of beetroot** with marigold petals and cool mint and garlic yoghurt relish ▪ **pissaladière** ▪ **root vegetable pie** ▪ **gratin of courgettes** with potatoes and tomatoes

chicken stew with parsley and cornmeal dumplings

This is a wonderful stew, made extra special by the star anise, and by the brilliant yellow, grainy dumplings flecked lavishly with green parsley.

SERVES 4

2 TABLESPOONS OLIVE OR SUNFLOWER OIL

1 RED ONION OR ORDINARY ONION, CUT INTO 8 WEDGES

3 CELERY STICKS, SLICED

1 FREE-RANGE CHICKEN, CUT INTO 8-10 PIECES

2 GARLIC CLOVES, CHOPPED

1 SMALL GLASS OF RED WINE

550 G (1 LB 2 OZ) TOMATO PASSATA

1 BOUQUET GARNI (CONSISTING OF 2 SPRIGS OF PARSLEY, 2 SPRIGS OF THYME, 1 SPRIG OF ROSEMARY AND 1 BAY LEAF)

1 STAR ANISE

SALT AND FRESHLY GROUND BLACK PEPPER

FOR THE DUMPLINGS:

85 G (3 OZ) QUICK-COOKING POLENTA OR FINE CORNMEAL

85 G (3 OZ) PLAIN FLOUR, SIFTED

2 TEASPOONS BAKING POWDER

60 G (2 OZ) BUTTER, MELTED

3 TABLESPOONS FINELY CHOPPED PARSLEY

2 GARLIC CLOVES, FINELY CHOPPED

METHOD

To make the stew, heat the oil over a high heat in a roomy casserole. Add the onion wedges and leave undisturbed for a couple of minutes to brown and caramelise, then scoop out and set aside. Now add the celery to the pan and sauté until patched with brown (this takes longer than you might imagine). Scoop out the celery and stash with the onion. Next, add the chicken to the pan and brown on both sides, then add the garlic and return the onion and celery to the pan. Add all the remaining ingredients and stir about. Cook down hard for 5 minutes, then add enough water to cover the chicken. Bring to the boil, then reduce the heat and simmer gently for about 40 minutes, until the chicken is cooked. If the sauce seems overly liquid and copious, boil down hard for another 5–10 minutes or so. Don't reduce it too much, though, as the dumplings will absorb some of the liquid. Taste and adjust the seasoning.

Meanwhile, make the dumplings. Mix the cornmeal, flour, baking powder and some salt, then mix in the melted butter, parsley, garlic and just enough water to form a soft, slightly sticky dough. Roll into hazelnut-sized balls. Drop the dumplings into the stew, cover with a lid and leave to simmer for 15 minutes, until the dumplings have puffed up and cooked through. Serve immediately.

daube of beef with cannellini beans and rosemary

One of the best cuts of beef for stewing just happens to be one of the cheapest. Shin of beef is veined with translucent folds between the muscle, which break down during long cooking to give a velvety richness to the sauce. I've called this stew a *daube* because it is flavoured with the scents of the *daubes*, or casseroles, of southern France – most notably, rosemary and dried orange zest. You'll be amazed at the power of one lone strip of dried orange zest, so much stronger than a fresh strip. Simply take a strip of zest off an orange and leave to dry overnight.

SERVES 4

225 G (8 OZ) DRIED CANNELLINI BEANS,
    SOAKED OVERNIGHT
1 ONION, CHOPPED
2 CARROTS, DICED
2 CELERY STALKS, DICED
2 TABLESPOONS OLIVE OIL
4 GARLIC CLOVES, CHOPPED
800-900 G (1¾-2 LB) SHIN OF BEEF, CUT INTO
    4 CM (1½ IN) CUBES
A BOUQUET GARNI MADE OF 1 BAY LEAF,
    3 SPRIGS OF ROSEMARY AND 1 STRIP OF
    DRIED ORANGE PEEL, TIED TOGETHER
    WITH STRING
600 ML (1 PINT) WATER
1 TABLESPOON TOMATO PURÉE
2 CANNED PLUM TOMATOES, ROUGHLY CHOPPED
SALT AND FRESHLY GROUND BLACK PEPPER

METHOD

Pre-heat the oven to 150°C/300°F/Gas Mark 2.

Drain the beans and rinse. Sauté the onion, carrots and celery in the oil until patched with brown. Add the garlic and cook for a minute or two longer. Place in an ovenproof casserole dish with the beans. Now brown the chunks of beef thoroughly in the remaining oil in the pan. Put them into the casserole as well, pushing them down among the beans and vegetables. Add the *bouquet garni* and season with pepper, but don't add any salt at this stage.

Pour any excess fat out of the frying pan, then pour in the water. Bring up to the boil, scraping in the residues from frying the meat and vegetables. When it is boiling, pour into the casserole and add enough hot water to just cover the meat. Transfer to the oven and leave to cook for about 2 hours. Stir, and taste one of the beans to see if it is completely tender. If it is still a bit firm, return the stew to the oven for another 30 minutes or so, then try again. Once the beans are tender, stir in the tomato purée, chopped tomatoes and some salt. Cook for a further 1–2 hours until the meat is incredibly tender. Taste and adjust the seasoning, then serve.

lancashire hotpot

Forget fancy dishes from the East and the Mediterranean; our own traditional, homely Lancashire hotpot makes a great meal on a cold evening. It is cheap, quick to prepare and lip-smackingly good. Once you've got it going in the oven, you don't need to bother about it for a couple of hours. No fussing or fiddling. I love it – there's a delicious crisp layer of potatoes on the top, covering tender lamb (or mutton if you can get it) and melting potatoes underneath that just beg to be mashed into the juices.

No doubt Lancastrians would debate the list of ingredients needed to make a genuine hotpot. I've read that mushrooms are added only in Bolton, and, in times past, oysters were frequently included as they were cheap and nutritious. I can think of better things to do with oysters these days, but mushrooms do add something special, and I always slip some in. You don't have to brown the meat, but it does improve the colour and flavour.

SERVES 6

6 MEATY LAMB LOIN CHOPS, OR 12 LAMB CUTLETS

6 LAMB'S KIDNEYS, HALVED

60 G (2 OZ) DRIPPING OR BUTTER, MELTED

1 KG (2 LB 4OZ) POTATOES, THINLY SLICED

3 LARGE ONIONS, SLICED

225 G (8 OZ) FLAT-CAP MUSHROOMS, THICKLY SLICED (OPTIONAL)

300 ML (½ PINT) LAMB OR CHICKEN STOCK, OR WATER

SALT AND FRESHLY GROUND BLACK PEPPER

METHOD

Pre-heat the oven to 220°C/425°F/Gas Mark 7.

Brown the chops and kidneys in half the dripping or butter over a high heat to give them a little colour. Layer the potatoes, chops, kidneys, onions and mushrooms, if using, in a deep casserole, seasoning well between each layer. End with a layer of potatoes, neatly overlapping and covering the contents of the dish. Pour over the stock or water. There should be enough to come about halfway up the ingredients. If you seem to be running short, add a little more water. Brush the remaining dripping or butter over the top layer of potatoes, then season well.

Cover the casserole and place it in the oven. Give it 20–25 minutes to heat through, then reduce the oven temperature to 150°C/300°F/Gas Mark 2 and leave to cook for a further 2 hours. Finally, remove the lid, raise the oven temperature back to 220°C/425°F/Gas Mark 7 and cook for a final 20–30 minutes until the top layer of potatoes is browned.

crown roast of pork with spiced prune and apricot stuffing

This is one of the most impressive joints you can serve, but do give your butcher ample notice as the pork will have to be cut from the carcass in a way that is slightly different from the norm (the rib bones are cut longer than usual). Allow plenty of time for cooking, too. Mine took a full 4½ hours!

The joint produces a fair amount of its own juices, but if you want to extend them, just deglaze the pan with wine, stock or even cider. You can't fit a huge amount of stuffing inside the crown, so, if you wish, double the quantity and bake the extra alongside the joint for the final 40 minutes.

SERVES 8 GREEDY PEOPLE OR 10 MORE ABSTEMIOUS ONES

1 PREPARED CROWN ROAST OF PORK WEIGHING ABOUT 3–3.5 KG (6½–8 LB)

FOR THE STUFFING:
6 PRUNES
6 DRIED APRICOTS
1 ONION, CHOPPED
30 G (1 OZ) BUTTER
1½ TEASPOONS BLACK MUSTARD SEEDS
1 TEASPOON CORIANDER SEEDS, COARSELY CRUSHED
1 LEVEL TEASPOON ANISEEDS
225 G (8 OZ) PORK SAUSAGEMEAT
85 G (3 OZ) SOFT BROWN BREADCRUMBS
SALT AND FRESHLY GROUND BLACK PEPPER

METHOD

Pre-heat the oven to 230°C/450°F/Gas Mark 8.

To make the stuffing, soak the prunes and apricots until soft, if necessary, then dry and chop them. Soften the onion in the butter until tender, then add the spices. Sauté until the mustard seeds begin to jump. Draw off the heat and mix with the dried fruit, sausagemeat, breadcrumbs, salt and pepper.

Weigh a roasting tin (you'll see why in a minute). Now grease the tin and stand the crown roast in it. Fill the central cavity with the stuffing, doming it up in the centre and gently pushing the meat into a nice circular crown. Weigh in the tin, then deduct the weight of the tin to get the weight of the stuffed crown. Calculate the roasting time by allowing 33 minutes per 450 g (30 minutes per lb) and 20 minutes extra. Protect the tips of the bones with twists of silver foil. After it has had 1½–2 hours in the oven you will also need to protect the stuffing from burning with a circle of foil.

Roast the crown at the pre-heated oven temperature for the first 15 minutes, then reduce it to 180°C/350°F/Gas Mark 4 for the remainder of the cooking time. Test to make sure the meat is cooked, then turn off the oven, open the door and leave the roast to relax for 25–30 minutes before carving.

roast rack of lamb
with a herb crust

There is no more perfect joint for two than a tender little rack of lamb. It doesn't come cheap, but for a special occasion it is worth every penny. The meat, cooked on the bone, has an excellent sweet flavour. The cooked rack looks pretty and it hardly takes any time to prepare and roast. This is my favourite way of cooking rack of lamb, with a crisp crust of buttery crumbs flavoured with lots of fresh herbs.

You can doll up the tips of the cutlets with cutlet frills (they're often sold with the rack, in which case do remember to take them off before the meat goes into the oven, replacing them just before serving).

SERVES 2

1 RACK OF LAMB

30 G (1 OZ) STALE FINE BREADCRUMBS

20 G (A GENEROUS ½ OZ) UNSALTED BUTTER, MELTED

1½–2 TABLESPOONS CHOPPED FRESH HERBS, SUCH AS A MIXTURE OF PARSLEY, CHERVIL, CHIVES, MARJORAM, THYME, SAVORY, ETC.

1 GARLIC CLOVE, CRUSHED

SALT AND FRESHLY GROUND BLACK PEPPER

METHOD

Pre-heat the oven to 230°C/450°F/Gas Mark 8.

If the rack hasn't already been prepared, carefully cut off the skin, leaving a thin layer of fat on the chops. Trim the tips of the cutlets, scraping away the scraps of meat and fat, exposing the top 4 cm (1½ in). Mix the breadcrumbs with the butter, herbs, garlic, salt and pepper in a bowl. Using your hands, keep turning the mixture over until the crumbs have soaked up all the butter evenly. Lay the rack of lamb, fat-side upward, in a lightly oiled, small ovenproof dish or roasting tin. Pat the crumb mixture firmly and thickly on to the fat side.

Roast the rack for about 20–30 minutes, depending on how well cooked you like your lamb (I usually opt for little more than 20 minutes since it seems a shame to overcook such a choice morsel). If necessary, cover the crumbs loosely with foil towards the end of the cooking time to prevent them from burning. Let the meat rest for 5 minutes, then, to serve, simply cut down between the cutlets, dividing the rack in half. It's best to do this at the table, as some of the crumbs are bound to fall off in the process and your fellow diner gets to see how appetizing it looks first.

moussaka

When it is made with care and high-quality ingredients, moussaka becomes one of the most delicious lamb dishes around. If you've been put off by tired, greasy restaurant slabs of moussaka, then I urge you to try your hand at home. It's not a dish to be rushed – the three elements take some time to prepare, but both sauces can quite happily be made a day in advance.

To cut down on the oil content, I bake the aubergine slices, brushed with just enough oil to keep them moist and add a little flavour (the traditional way is to fry them). You could do away with the oil on the aubergines altogether by steaming them, but I think you then lose out on too much flavour. As is so often the case, compromise is the best option. Whichever way you cook them, do it on the day the moussaka is to be eaten.

Try to get proper Greek kefalotyri cheese if you can (most Greek food stores stock it), as its rich tang suits this production to a T. If you don't have the right-sized dish, use one that is slightly smaller, so that you still get a decent thickness.

SERVES 6

3 LARGE OR 4 MEDIUM AUBERGINES, SLICED LENGTHWAYS

OLIVE OIL

60 G (2 OZ) KEFALOTYRI CHEESE,
    OR A MIXTURE OF GRUYÈRE AND PARMESAN

GENEROUS ½ TEASPOON GROUND CINNAMON

SALT AND FRESHLY GROUND BLACK PEPPER

FOR THE MEAT SAUCE:

1 LARGE ONION, CHOPPED

2 GARLIC CLOVES, CHOPPED

3 TABLESPOONS OLIVE OIL

450 G (1 LB) MINCED LAMB

1 GENEROUS GLASS OF DRY WHITE WINE

2 TABLESPOONS TOMATO PURÉE

450 G (1 LB) TOMATOES, SKINNED AND ROUGHLY CHOPPED

1 TEASPOON SUGAR

1½ TEASPOONS GROUND CINNAMON

1 TABLESPOON DRIED OREGANO

3 TABLESPOONS CHOPPED PARSLEY

FOR THE WHITE SAUCE:

60 G (2 OZ) BUTTER

60 G (2 OZ) FLOUR

600 ML (1 PINT) MILK

60 G (2 OZ) KEFALOTYRI CHEESE,
    OR MIXED PARMESAN AND GRUYÈRE, GRATED

1 EGG

1 EGG YOLK

METHOD

To make the meat sauce, cook the onion and garlic gently in the olive oil until tender, without browning. Add the lamb and stir until it loses its raw look. Now add all the remaining meat sauce ingredients except the parsley and season with salt and pepper. Simmer for 20–30 minutes until thick. Stir in the parsley.

Next, make the white sauce. Melt the butter and stir in the flour. Keep stirring for about 1 minute. Draw the pan off the heat and add the milk gradually, stirring in well between sploshes. Once you've incorporated about one-third of it, increase the amount you add each time. Return to a gentle heat and let it simmer for a good 10–15 minutes, stirring frequently, until it is fairly thick. Remove from the heat, stir in the cheese and salt and pepper. If not using immediately, spear a knob of butter on a fork and rub over the surface to prevent a skin forming. Reheat the white sauce gently when needed. Just before using, beat the egg and yolk into the sauce.

Sprinkle the slices of aubergine with salt and leave for at least 30 minutes, preferably a full hour. Wipe clean and steam if you wish, or lay them on oiled baking sheets, brush quite generously with olive oil and bake in the oven at 190°C/375°F/Gas Mark 5 for about 20 minutes until tender and patched with brown.

Take a rectangular or square baking dish, about 30 x 20 cm (12 x 8 in) or 25 x 25 cm (10 x 10 in), and brush lightly with oil. Lay half the aubergine slices on the base, overlapping if necessary, then spread half the meat sauce on top. Repeat these layers, then spoon over the white sauce, covering the meat entirely. Sprinkle the grated cheese and cinnamon on top. Bake at 180°C/350°F/Gas Mark 4 for 50–60 minutes until nicely browned. Let it settle, out of the oven, for 5 minutes before cutting into squares and serving.

pan-fried venison with port and orange sauce

A quick but elegant way to deal with plain venison chops. Dried sour cherries are now available from several of the smarter supermarkets and delis and have a marvellous flavour. If you can't get any, you could substitute large raisins or even a handful of little currants. It won't be quite the same, but it will still taste fine.

I've used this recipe both for venison chops and for prime venison saddle steaks. Quantities will vary according to cut and variety of deer, so you'll have to use your head when it comes to buying. The butcher should be able to advise you if you are ordering in advance.

SERVES 4

60 G (2 OZ) DRIED SOUR CHERRIES

JUICE OF 1 ORANGE

8 SMALL VENISON CHOPS, OR 8 SMALL SADDLE STEAKS (SEE ABOVE)

30 G (1 OZ) BUTTER

1 TABLESPOON OIL

1 SHALLOT, VERY FINELY CHOPPED

150 ML (¼ PINT) PORT

150 ML (¼ PINT) VENISON, BEEF OR CHICKEN STOCK

2 TABLESPOONS REDCURRANT JELLY

½ TEASPOON DIJON MUSTARD

SALT AND FRESHLY GROUND BLACK PEPPER

METHOD

Soak the dried cherries in the orange juice for 30 minutes. Dry the chops or steaks. Heat the butter and oil in a pan over a moderate heat. Fry the chops in the fat for about 5–8 minutes on each side, until cooked almost to your liking, then set aside. Add the shallot to the pan and cook gently, until tender. Drain the excess fat from the pan, then deglaze with the port, bringing it up to the boil and scraping in the residues from the pan. Let it bubble until reduced almost to nothing, then add the stock, orange juice and cherries. Boil until reduced by half. Now stir in the redcurrant jelly and mustard. Stir until the redcurrant jelly has dissolved into the sauce. Taste and adjust the seasoning, then spoon a little over and around the chops and serve the rest of the sauce alongside.

chez nous shepherd's pie

This is basically a classic shepherd's pie, made with cooked lamb (though you can also use raw minced lamb if that is more convenient) but flavoured liberally with fresh marjoram and garlic and moistened with red wine and tomatoes, just to give it a little more zip. It is a great favourite of ours and perfect comfort food on a cold day.

SERVES 4 VERY HUNGRY PEOPLE OR 6 ORDINARY MORTALS

1 ONION, CHOPPED

1 RED PEPPER, SEEDED AND FINELY DICED

1 LARGE CARROT, FINELY DICED

2 TABLESPOONS SUNFLOWER OIL

2-3 GARLIC CLOVES, CHOPPED

350-400 G (12-14 OZ) RARE ROAST LAMB, THINLY SLICED THEN FINELY DICED,
   OR MINCED RAW LAMB

1 SMALL SPRIG OF ROSEMARY (OPTIONAL)

400 G (14 OZ) CAN CHOPPED TOMATOES

150 ML (¼ PINT) RED WINE

1 TABLESPOON WORCESTERSHIRE SAUCE

2 TABLESPOONS CHOPPED MARJORAM OR 1-1½ TEASPOONS DRIED OREGANO

SALT AND FRESHLY GROUND BLACK PEPPER

FOR THE TOPPING:

1 KG (2 LB 4 OZ) LARGE POTATOES IN THEIR SKINS

45 G (1½ OZ) BUTTER

150 ML (¼ PINT) MILK

METHOD

Start by making the topping. Either bake the potatoes in their skins or microwave them until tender, in which case remember to prick the skins first so that they don't burst all over the microwave. Cut in half while still hot and scoop out the insides. While it is still hot, mash the potato with two-thirds of the butter and some salt, gradually working in the milk to give a smooth mash.

Fry the onion, pepper and carrot in the oil over a moderate heat until the onion and pepper are tender. Add the garlic and continue cooking for a minute or two. If you are using roast lamb, add to the pan now. If you are using raw minced lamb, raise the heat high, then add the lamb and fry for 5 minutes or so at a rollicking heat, breaking up the lumps, until it is lightly coloured all over. Now add the rosemary if you are using raw mince, or if you did not flavour the roast with rosemary. Stir in the tomatoes, wine and Worcestershire sauce and season well. Bring up to the boil and then leave to simmer gently for at least 45 minutes if it was roast lamb, or at least 1 hour if it was raw lamb. If necessary, add a little hot water to prevent it drying out. Stir in the marjoram when the sauce is more or less cooked. By the time it is done, the mixture should be moist, rich and a darkish brown, and definitely not swimming in liquid. Taste and adjust the seasoning.

Pre-heat the oven to around 220°C/425°F/Gas Mark 7 (a little less won't hurt if you have something else cooking in there at the same time).

Spread the mince out in an ovenproof dish to give a layer about 2–2.5 cm (¾–1 in) thick. Dot the mashed potato on top, then smooth down carefully, spreading it right to the sides. Use a fork to make waves or swirls or whatever pattern takes your fancy on the top of the potato. Dot with the remaining butter. Pop the dish into the oven and leave to reheat and brown for 25–30 minutes. Serve steaming hot and full of comfort.

cauliflower and tomato crumble

This recipe transforms cauliflower into a more substantial offering, with a savoury crumble topping that browns appetizingly in the heat of the oven. For a wetter dish, moisten the cauliflower in a bechamel sauce or tomato sauce before covering with the crumble mixture. Serve as a main or first course.

SERVES 4-6

1 HEAD OF CAULIFLOWER, BROKEN INTO FLORETS

4 TOMATOES, SLICED

1 TEASPOON FRESH THYME LEAVES OR ½ TEASPOON DRIED

30 G (1 OZ) BUTTER

SALT AND FRESHLY GROUND BLACK PEPPER

FOR THE CRUMBLE:

115 G (4 OZ) PLAIN FLOUR

60 G (2 OZ) ROLLED OATS

60 G (2 OZ) CHEDDAR CHEESE, GRATED

115 G (4 OZ) BUTTER

SALT AND FRESHLY GROUND BLACK PEPPER

METHOD

Cook the cauliflower in salted, boiling water, or steam, until almost tender. Pack tightly in a lightly buttered, heatproof dish. Cover with tomato slices. Sprinkle with thyme leaves, salt and pepper, then dot with the butter.

Pre-heat the oven to 200°C/400°F/Gas Mark 6.

To make the crumble, mix the flour, oats and grated cheese with some salt and pepper in a bowl. Melt the butter and stir enough of it into the mixture with a palette knife to make a crumbly mixture. Cool slightly, then scatter over the vegetables in a thick layer. Bake for about 30 minutes, until the crumble is golden brown and crisp. Serve immediately.

chicken with tarragon

Tarragon-scented roast chicken with a creamy sauce makes a perfect Sunday lunch main-piece. To enjoy it at its best you will need a real free-range bird, with flesh that has some flavour and resistance to it. The tarragon, stuffed into its body cavity and in the sauce, has such a strong affinity with chicken that it is surprising we don't use them together more. However, that doesn't mean you should go overboard with the herb. It's fairly powerful and a little goes a fair old way. The amount I've added to the sauce seems about right to me, though since all herbs vary in intensity, you may want to add a little more. Keep tasting (no problem in this case, as long as you don't guzzle more than your fair share) to get it right.

SERVES 4

1.8 KG (4 LB) FREE-RANGE CHICKEN

½ LEMON

4 BRANCHES OF TARRAGON

60 G (2 OZ) UNSALTED BUTTER

50 ML (2 FL OZ) VERMOUTH, OR A SMALL GLASS OF DRY WHITE WINE

300 ML (½ PINT) CRÈME FRAÎCHE OR DOUBLE CREAM

LEMON JUICE

SALT AND FRESHLY GROUND BLACK PEPPER

METHOD

Pre-heat the oven to 200°C/400°F/Gas Mark 6.

Rub the skin of the chicken all over with the lemon half. Stuff the spent lemon half into the stomach cavity of the chicken along with 3 of the branches of tarragon. Chop the leaves of the remaining tarragon, discarding the stalk. Sit the bird in a roasting tin, smear the butter thickly over its skin and season generously with salt and pepper. Roast for 1–1¼ hours, until cooked through. Transfer the bird to a serving dish and let it rest in the oven with the heat turned off and the door ajar, while you make the sauce.

Skim off as much fat as you can from the roasting tin, leaving behind the roasting juices. Put the tin on the hob and pour in the vermouth or wine. Bring up to the boil, scraping in any residues from roasting, and boil until reduced to a few spoonfuls. Now add the cream and stir, and let it return to the boil. Continue to cook hard until reduced to a good consistency. Draw off the heat and add 2–3 teaspoons of the chopped tarragon. Season with salt and pepper and a dash of lemon juice. Taste and adjust the seasoning, then serve the sauce with the chicken.

porc aux pruneaux de tours

The area around Tours in western France was once famed for its prunes, though now prune drying is history. Prunes, however, linger on in the local repertoire. The classier pâtisseries make wicked *pruneaux fourrés*, stuffed with apricot and almond pastes and glazed with apricot gel, then there's the unlikely sounding but absolutely delicious *matelote d'anguilles* – prune and eel stew – and this dish of pork cooked with prunes, the local wine and lots of cream.

When I was a child we spent every summer in this area and on highdays and holidays my mother would often make us Porc aux Pruneaux de Tours. Though it can be made with cheaper cuts of pork and is all too often drowned in a floury wine sauce, the best recipe, and by far the easiest, is this one, largely my mother's version, though with a few more prunes (I love them!) and a little less cream. It is a fabulous dish for a dinner party, particularly mid-week when cooking and preparation time is at a premium. If you remember, put the prunes to soak the night before, even if they are of the soft, no-soak, ready-to-eat variety.

SERVES 4

24 PRUNES

300 ML (½ PINT) VOUVRAY OR OTHER DRY WHITE WINE

2 PORK FILLETS (TENDERLOINS)

60 G (2 OZ) BUTTER

SEASONED FLOUR, FOR DUSTING

1 LEVEL TABLESPOON REDCURRANT JELLY

300 ML (½ PINT) WHIPPING CREAM

A SQUEEZE OF LEMON JUICE

SALT AND FRESHLY GROUND BLACK PEPPER

METHOD

Soak the prunes in the wine for as long as possible – at least an hour, but if you have time, leave them overnight. Slit open the prunes and remove their stones. Reserve the prunes and don't throw out the wine!

Slice each tenderloin thickly into 9 discs (that's 18 altogether). Heat the butter in a wide frying pan until it is foaming, dust the pieces of pork with seasoned flour and fry over a moderate heat until just tender. If necessary, do this in two batches so as not to overcrowd the pan. Slices of fillet don't take very long – about 4 minutes on each side. Remove from the pan, arrange on a serving dish and keep warm.

Pour any excess fat from the pan, return to the heat and pour in the wine from soaking the prunes. Bring up to the boil, scraping in all the meaty residues. Stir in the redcurrant jelly, then boil hard over a high heat until reduced to a syrupy consistency.

Now stir in the cream and reduce the sauce until nicely thickened. When it is almost done, pop in the prunes to warm through. Finally add a splash of lemon juice to heighten the flavours and season with salt and pepper. Dot the prunes around the pork and pour over the sauce. Serve at once.

roast cod with a coriander crust

This use of coriander in a breadcrumb crust is the kind of thing that has become very fashionable in Britain over recent years. If you can lay your hands on a really fresh bit of cod, this recipe will show it off at its very best.

SERVES 4

675 G (1 LB 8 OZ) FRESHEST COD FILLET

85 G (3 OZ) SOFT OR SLIGHTLY STALE WHITE BREADCRUMBS

3 GENEROUS TABLESPOONS CHOPPED FRESH CORIANDER

3 GARLIC CLOVES, CRUSHED

FINELY GRATED ZEST OF ½ LEMON

60 G (2 OZ) BUTTER, MELTED

LEMON WEDGES, TO SERVE

SALT AND FRESHLY GROUND BLACK PEPPER

METHOD

Pre-heat the oven to 220°C/425°F/Gas Mark 7.

Season the cod with salt and pepper. Mix the breadcrumbs with the coriander, garlic, lemon zest, salt and pepper and then add the butter and mix thoroughly with your fingers. Place the cod in a shallow, ovenproof dish and press the buttered crumbs firmly on to the cod to form an even crust. Bake for 20–30 minutes, until the crust is browned and the fish just about cooked through. Serve immediately with lemon wedges.

laksa lemak

Laksa Lemak, from Singapore, is one of my all-time favourite South-east Asian dishes. In fact, it is possibly one of my all-time favourite dishes full stop. A *laksa* is a spicy soup and there are many variations. The Singaporean *laksa* is rich with coconut milk and aswim with rice noodles, prawns and occasionally other seafood. A true *laksa* will be flavoured with laksa leaf, but if you can't find any, coriander will have to do instead.

It is not a quick dish to make, though the broth can be made in advance, then all you need do is reheat it and finish by adding the more substantial ingredients that take only a few minutes to cook. For a special occasion, it really is worth taking the trouble.

SERVES 6

6 LARGE SCALLOPS

250 G (9 OZ) RAW PRAWNS IN THEIR SHELLS

1 TABLESPOON GROUNDNUT, VEGETABLE OR SUNFLOWER OIL

500 G (1 LB 2 OZ) MUSSELS

400 ML (14 FL OZ) COCONUT MILK

1-2 TABLESPOONS FISH SAUCE

400 G (14 OZ) FRESH FLAT RICE NOODLES

3 KAFFIR LIME LEAVES, VERY FINELY SHREDDED,
   OR 2 WIDE STRIPS OF LIME ZEST

115 G (4 OZ) BEANSPROUTS

A HANDFUL OF LAKSA LEAVES OR CORIANDER LEAVES, ROUGHLY CHOPPED

LIME WEDGES, TO SERVE

FOR THE SPICE PASTE:

3 LEMON GRASS STEMS

3 RED CHILLIES, SEEDED AND CHOPPED

2 GARLIC CLOVES, CHOPPED

2.5 CM (1 IN) FRESH GALANGAL OR ROOT GINGER, CHOPPED

4 SHALLOTS, THINLY SLICED

1 TABLESPOON ANCHOVY ESSENCE OR ANCHOVY PASTE

3 TABLESPOONS GROUNDNUT, SUNFLOWER OR VEGETABLE OIL

1 TEASPOON GROUND TURMERIC

1 TABLESPOON GROUND CORIANDER

METHOD

Remove the dark vein that is sometimes left on the scallops. Separate the corals and the whites, then cut each white into 2–3 discs, according to size. Peel the prawns, saving the shells and heads. If necessary, make a little slit with the tip of a sharp knife down the back of each prawn, then remove the fine black gut that sometimes lies just below the surface. Set the prawns aside. Fry the shells and heads in the oil until pink. Add about 1.7 litres (3 pints) of water, bring up to the boil and simmer for 30 minutes. Strain and discard the shells. Boil the stock down until reduced to 1.2 litres (2 pints).

While the stock is simmering, rinse the mussels thoroughly, scrape off any barnacles and cut away the beards. Rinse again. Discard any mussels that will not close when rapped firmly on the work surface. Pour 300 ml (½ pint) of water into a large saucepan. Bring to the boil, add the mussels, cover tightly and shake over a high heat until opened – this should take no more than a few minutes. Any mussels that refuse to open must be discarded. Lift the mussels out, then strain the cooking juices to remove grit. Reserve the juices. Take about two-thirds of the mussels out of their shells and set aside.

For the spice paste, slice off and discard the upper half of the lemon grass stems, leaving just the lower 7.5–10 cm (3–4 in). Slice thinly into little rounds and put into a food processor with the chillies, garlic, galangal or ginger, shallots, anchovy essence or paste and about 2 tablespoons of water. Process to a paste, adding a touch more water if necessary to lubricate. Heat the oil in a heavy pan and add the paste. Fry, stirring continuously and scraping the bottom of the pan to prevent burning, until browned – allow about 15 minutes. Now add the turmeric and coriander and fry for a further minute or so. Next add the prawn stock and the liquor from cooking the mussels. Bring up to the boil and simmer for 10 minutes.

Add the coconut milk and fish sauce, bring back to the boil, then push in the noodles. Once softened, add the kaffir lime leaves and simmer for 2 minutes. Tip in the prawns and simmer for 2 more minutes. Add the scallops, stir, then add the shelled mussels and beansprouts. Give everything one final stir.

To serve, spoon into big, deep bowls and perch the mussels in their shells on top. Scatter with laksa leaves or coriander and tuck a lime wedge neatly on top, to be squeezed over just before slurping it all down.

chicken with jerusalem artichoke stuffing

A well-flavoured roast chicken – free-range, not broiler – with a good stuffing makes a first-class main course for Sunday lunch. Nuggets of Jerusalem artichoke give this stuffing a most appetizing flavour. If you have the choice, pick out Jerusalem artichokes that are as smooth as possible, which will make them easier to peel.

SERVES 4

1.3–1.8 KG (3–4 LB) CHICKEN

15 G (½ OZ) BUTTER

SALT AND FRESHLY GROUND BLACK PEPPER

FOR THE STUFFING:

450 G (1 LB) JERUSALEM ARTICHOKES

30 G (1 OZ) BUTTER

2 RASHERS RINDLESS BACON, DICED

1 SMALL ONION, FINELY CHOPPED

1 SPRIG OF THYME

2 TABLESPOONS CHOPPED PARSLEY

85 G (3 OZ) SOFT BROWN BREADCRUMBS

3 SPRING ONIONS, CHOPPED

2 TEASPOONS CHOPPED TARRAGON

½ TEASPOON WORCESTERSHIRE SAUCE

1 EGG, BEATEN

METHOD

To make the stuffing, boil the artichokes in their skins until just tender, but not soggy. Cool slightly and peel, then chop finely.

Melt the butter in a pan and add the bacon, onion (not the spring onions), thyme and parsley. Cover and sweat for 10 minutes.

Remove the lid and raise the heat. Cook, stirring occasionally, until virtually all the liquid has evaporated. Cool slightly. Mix with the artichokes, bread-crumbs, spring onions, tarragon, Worcestershire sauce, salt and pepper, then add enough beaten egg to bind.

Preheat the oven to 200°C/400°F/Gas Mark 6. Fill the chicken with the stuffing. Rub the butter into the skin and season with salt and pepper. Roast, basting occasionally, for 1¼–1½ hours until the chicken juices run clear. Turn off the heat. Rest the chicken for 10 minutes in the oven with the door slightly ajar, before carving.

monkfish with garlic and rosemary

A skinned and beheaded tail of monkfish bears a passing resemblance to a leg of lamb and is sometimes known, therefore, as a *gigot*. The piscine *gigot* can, as it happens, be cooked in a similar fashion to the meaty one, studded with slivers of garlic and needles of rosemary, then roasted in a hot oven.

SERVES 4-6

900 G-1.5 KG (2-3 LB) MONKFISH TAIL

2 GARLIC CLOVES, CUT INTO FINE SHARDS

LEAVES OF 1 SMALL SPRIG OF ROSEMARY

1 RED ONION, THINLY SLICED

1 GLASS OF DRY WHITE WINE

125 ML (4 FL OZ) EXTRA VIRGIN OLIVE OIL

SALT AND LOADS OF FRESHLY GROUND BLACK PEPPER

METHOD

Pre-heat the oven to 190°C/375°F/Gas Mark 5.

Make slits all over the monkfish tail and push in slivers of garlic and rosemary leaves, using the handle of a teaspoon or some other thin, blunt instrument.

Place the onion slices in an ovenproof dish and sit the monkfish on top. Pour over the wine and oil, then season with salt and pepper. Roast for 25–30 minutes, until just cooked through, basting occasionally with the pan juices.

pilaff of beetroot
with marigold petals and cool mint
and garlic yoghurt relish

The dark red of the beetroot coupled with the turmeric and marigold yellows transforms this into one of the most vibrantly coloured rice dishes you are likely to come across – echoing the rich, deep hues of Moorish art. The taste, too, is rich and vibrant – a perfect dish for a vegetarian main course, or for a side dish with plainly cooked meats or grilled spicy sausages.

SERVES 4-6

30 G (1 OZ) BUTTER

1 TABLESPOON OLIVE, SUNFLOWER OR VEGETABLE OIL

1 ONION, CHOPPED

2 GARLIC CLOVES, CHOPPED

½ TABLESPOON CUMIN SEEDS

2 CLOVES

1 CINNAMON STICK

250 G (9 OZ) BASMATI OR LONG-GRAIN RICE, RINSED AND DRAINED

1 LEVEL TEASPOON GROUND TURMERIC

550 ML (19 FL OZ) WATER

250 G (9 OZ) BEETROOT, COOKED, PEELED AND CUT INTO 1 CM (½ IN) DICE

PETALS OF 2-3 MARIGOLD FLOWERS

SALT AND FRESHLY GROUND BLACK PEPPER

FOR THE YOGHURT RELISH:

2 GARLIC CLOVES, CHOPPED

15 G (½ OZ) BUTTER

250 G (9 OZ) GREEK YOGHURT

2 TABLESPOONS CHOPPED MINT

1 TABLESPOON CHOPPED CHIVES (OPTIONAL)

METHOD

To make the pilaff, heat the butter with the oil in a saucepan, then add the onion and fry gently, until translucent. Add the garlic, cumin seeds, cloves and cinnamon and fry gently for 1 minute. Now tip in the rice and stir for 1 further minute, until slightly translucent. Stir in the turmeric, then add the water and some salt and pepper and bring to the boil. Cover and cook for 8 minutes over a very low heat. Stir in the beetroot, then cover again and leave, without stirring, for 5–8 minutes, until all the liquid has been absorbed and the rice is tender. Set aside a few of the marigold petals for decoration and stir the rest in. Taste and adjust the seasoning, then tip into a warmed serving dish, cover and leave in a low oven (110°C/225°F/Gas Mark ¼) for 10–30 minutes to dry. Just before serving, sprinkle over the remaining marigold petals.

To make the yoghurt relish, fry the garlic in the butter until very lightly browned. Scoop out and stir into the yoghurt with the herbs and some salt to taste. Serve at room temperature, to spoon on to the pilaff.

pissaladière

Pissaladière is made throughout Provence and parts of northern Italy, but it belongs above all to Nice, where you can buy big squares of it, wrapped in a piece of waxed paper, to eat as you walk through the streets.

Although it is often made with a bread dough, more like a pizza, I prefer a shortcrust base. The sweetness of the slowly cooked onion and the saltiness of anchovies and olives is set off to perfection by the crumbly texture of the pastry. Some recipes for Pissaladière mix tomato with the onion and, good though they are, I think the simpler onion-only topping better. Save the tomatoes to make a salad to serve alongside.

Pissaladière is perfect for a summer lunch, supper party, or for a picnic. It can be eaten still warm, or cold, as a main course or cut into smaller squares as a starter.

SERVES 6-8 AS A MAIN COURSE

350 G (12 OZ) SHORTCRUST PASTRY (SEE PAGE 141)

FLOUR, FOR DUSTING

FOR THE FILLING:

3 TABLESPOONS OLIVE OIL

1 KG (2 LB 4 OZ) ONIONS, THINLY SLICED

2 GARLIC CLOVES, FINELY CHOPPED

3 SPRIGS OF FRESH THYME OR ½ TEASPOON DRIED

2 SPRIGS OF FRESH ROSEMARY OR 1 TEASPOON DRIED

1 BAY LEAF

2 SPRIGS OF FRESH PARSLEY

60 G (2 OZ) BLACK OLIVES (PREFERABLY NIÇOISE), PITTED

1 CAN ANCHOVY FILLETS, DRAINED AND HALVED LENGTHWAYS

SALT AND FRESHLY GROUND BLACK PEPPER

METHOD

Roll out the pastry on a lightly floured board to form a rectangle large enough to line a 28 x 30 cm (9 x 12 in) baking tray. Line the tray with the pastry, prick the base with a fork, then cover and rest in the fridge for 30 minutes to 1 hour while you prepare the filling.

Warm the oil in a saucepan large enough to take all the onions. Add the onions, garlic, herbs and a little salt and pepper. Cover tightly and stew gently over a low heat for 30–40 minutes, stirring occasionally, until the onions are meltingly tender. Discard the herbs. Cool slightly and add plenty of pepper (no more salt, as the olives and anchovies will ensure that there is no shortage).

Put a baking tray, the same size as the one lined with pastry, in the oven and heat to 200°C/400°F/Gas Mark 6. Spread the onion thickly on the pastry, arrange the anchovy fillets in a lattice on top and place an olive in the centre of each diamond. Sit the pissaladière on the hot baking tray in the oven (this helps give a crisper base), and bake for 20–25 minutes until browned. Serve cut into squares, hot, warm or cold.

root vegetable pie

This sturdy root vegetable pie wrapped in puff pastry makes a magnificent main course without breaking the bank. It's one of those recipes that somehow seems to exceed the sum of its parts, tasting ten times better than you might expect.

SERVES 4–6

450 G (1 LB) CARROTS, SLICED

450 G (1 LB) POTATOES, SLICED

225 G (8 OZ) TURNIPS, PEELED IF NECESSARY AND SLICED

450 G (1 LB) PUFF PASTRY, THAWED IF FROZEN

FLOUR, FOR DUSTING

2 TABLESPOONS FINELY CHOPPED PARSLEY

2 TEASPOONS CARAWAY SEEDS

SALT AND FRESHLY GROUND BLACK PEPPER

60 G (2 OZ) BUTTER, PLUS EXTRA FOR GREASING

1 EGG, BEATEN

METHOD

Bring a large pan of lightly salted water to the boil. Cook the carrot slices for 6 minutes, then scoop out and drain. Repeat with the potatoes and turnips, keeping each vegetable separate.

Butter a loose-bottomed cake tin 5 cm (2 in) deep and 20 cm (8 in) in diameter. Roll out two-thirds of the pastry on a lightly floured surface to give a rough circle of about 33 cm (13 in) in diameter. Loosely fold in half, then in quarters, then lift into the tin with the centre tip of the pastry at the centre of the tin. Carefully unfold, then lift the edges and gently push the pastry down to line the sides of the tin, using a small knob of pastry rolled into a ball to ease it right into the corners.

Make separate layers of potatoes, carrots and turnips, sprinkling parsley, caraway seeds and salt and pepper between the layers and dotting with butter as you go.

Roll out the remaining pastry and lay over the pie. Trim off the excess and press the edges of the pastry together firmly. Make a hole in the centre, then let the pie rest for 30 minutes in the fridge.

Pre-heat the oven to 220°C/425°F/ Gas Mark 7. Brush the top of the pie with beaten egg and bake for 10 minutes until golden brown. Reduce the oven temperature to 180°C/350°F/Gas Mark 4 and cook for a further 50–60 minutes. Test with a skewer to check that the vegetables are cooked and tender. Un-mould carefully and serve hot or warm.

gratin of courgettes
with potatoes and tomatoes

This gratin looks enchantingly pretty with its closely packed bands of green, red and white, patched with brown in the heat of the oven. As the vegetables cook they will shrink, so it is important to pack them tightly into the baking dish. Overlap them snugly, leaving only about 5 mm (¼ in) of each slice peeking out. That way, you will get a good balance of tenderness to crispness.

SERVES 4

225 G (8 OZ) TOMATOES

225 G (8 OZ) COURGETTES

225 G (8 OZ) WAXY POTATOES

1 MEDIUM RED ONION

½ TABLESPOON DRIED OREGANO

3 TABLESPOONS OLIVE OIL

SALT AND FRESHLY GROUND BLACK PEPPER

METHOD

Slice the tomatoes and courgettes into discs about 5 mm (¼ in) thick, then sprinkle them lightly with salt and leave for 30 minutes. Wipe dry. Peel the potatoes and slice them thinly. Halve the onion lengthways and slice each half thinly.

Pre-heat the oven to 180°C/350°F/Gas Mark 4.

Arrange the vegetables in a single closely-overlapping layer like the tiles on a roof, alternating potatoes, tomatoes, courgettes and onion, in an oiled heatproof dish. Season lightly with salt but add plenty of pepper. Sprinkle the oregano over the top and drizzle with olive oil.

Bake for about 50–60 minutes, until the potatoes are tender. As the gratin cooks, baste 2 or 3 times with its juices, trying not to disturb the arrangement too much. If the gratin threatens to burn, cover with foil towards the end of the cooking time. Serve hot.

4
tea and high tea

watercress sandwiches with chilli lemon butter ■ **smoked salmon** with lovage cream cheese on bagels ■ **potato pizza** with anchovies, mascarpone and rocket ■ **three-tomato tart** with marjoram ■ **himmel und erde** ■ **asparagus and gruyère quiche** ■ **fish gratin** ■ **sun-dried tomato bread** ■ **saffron teabread** ■ **banana teabread** ■ **polenta syrup cake** ■ **lavender shortbread** ■ sweet rice **fritters** ■ **rice pudding** brulée ■ margaret pover's **moist lemon cake** ■ betty skelly's **chocolate cake** ■ **hungarian pancakes** ■ violet graham's **scones** ■ **fig jam**

watercress sandwiches
with chilli lemon butter

Watercress sandwiches are one of the great delights of the world, in the same vein as and every bit as good as cucumber sandwiches. We used to have them for supper when I was a child. My father thought they should be made with white bread, but I preferred them with brown and still do. Brown or white, they have to be made with butter, not margarine, and you should pack a really generous quantity of watercress between the slices. No point in being stingy.

Even better than plain butter is this flavoured butter. Quite how far the 60 g (2 oz) of flavoured butter will go depends on the size of the slices of bread, but there should be ample for at least three sandwiches and probably four.

MAKES 3-4 SANDWICHES

1 BUNCH OF WATERCRESS

6-8 THIN SLICES OF WHOLEMEAL OR GRANARY BREAD

FOR THE BUTTER:

60 G (2 OZ) LIGHTLY SALTED BUTTER, SOFTENED

½ FRESH GREEN CHILLI, SEEDED AND VERY FINELY CHOPPED

FINELY GRATED ZEST OF ½ LEMON

1 TABLESPOON LEMON JUICE

METHOD

To make the butter, process all the butter ingredients together. If you don't have or don't feel like using a processor, make sure that the chilli is very finely chopped indeed, then mash all the ingredients together well with a fork. If you don't want to use the butter immediately, cover and store in the fridge until needed. Bring back to room temperature before using.

Pick over and wash the watercress and remove any damaged leaves. Butter the bread fairly generously. Heap the watercress up really thickly on 3 or 4 slices and then clamp the upper slices down firmly, pressing into place. Cut in half and eat.

smoked salmon
with lovage cream cheese on bagels

Smoked salmon and cream cheese are, in my opinion, a match made in heaven and this alternative sandwich makes a perfect treat for afternoon tea.

SERVES 3

3 BAGELS, SPLIT OPEN

4 TABLESPOONS CREAM CHEESE

1 TABLESPOON CHOPPED LOVAGE LEAVES

2 TEASPOONS CREAMED HORSERADISH (OPTIONAL)

LOTS OF SLICED SMOKED SALMON

FRESHLY GROUND BLACK PEPPER

METHOD

Toast the cut sides of the bagels, if you wish. Mash the cream cheese with the lovage and horseradish, if using, and smear thickly over the cut sides of the bagels. Sandwich as much smoked salmon as is humanly decent (or available) between the two halves of each bagel, seasoning generously with freshly ground black pepper. Eat greedily.

potato pizza with anchovies, mascarpone and rocket

Home-made pizzas are a real treat, and a cheap one too. They beat most takeaway pizzas hands down. This one is right up there at the top of the smart pizza list, with not a drop of tomato sauce in sight. Since the rest of the ingredients are incredibly cheap, you can afford to splash out on mascarpone, anchovies and fresh green rocket, which wilts a little in the heat of the pizza, giving a wonderful combination of peppery freshness and softened greens.

SERVES 2

1 LARGE POTATO (ABOUT 300 G/10 OZ)
6 CANNED ANCHOVY FILLETS, CUT IN HALF LENGTHWAYS
3 TABLESPOONS MASCARPONE CHEESE
OLIVE OIL
85–100 G (3–3½ OZ) ROCKET
SALT AND FRESHLY GROUND BLACK PEPPER

FOR THE DOUGH:
400 G (14 OZ) STRONG WHITE FLOUR, PLUS EXTRA FOR DUSTING
2 LEVEL TEASPOONS SALT
7 G SACHET OF EASY-BLEND YEAST
2 TABLESPOONS OLIVE OIL

METHOD

To make the dough, mix the flour, salt and yeast together in a bowl and make a well in the centre. Add the olive oil and enough water to mix to a soft, very slightly sticky dough – anything from 150–300 ml (¼–½ pint). Flour your hands and then gather the dough up into a ball. Knead vigorously on a lightly floured work surface for a good 8–10 minutes, until satin-smooth and elastic (or use the dough hook of an electric mixer at a low speed). Rinse the bowl out, then dry it and dust with flour. Place the dough in the bowl, turn to coat lightly in the flour, then cover with a damp cloth and leave in a warm place for about an hour or until it has doubled in size.

Peel the potato, then slice it paper-thin either in a food processor or on a mandoline. This is the key to the pizza – if the potato is too thick, it will not have time to cook through. Drop the potato slices into a bowl of cold water until needed.

Pre-heat the oven to 240°C/475°F/Gas Mark 9 or as high as it will go. Put 2 baking trays in the oven to heat through.

Return to the dough and punch it down. Gather up and knead again for a few minutes. Divide in half. Using your hands and/or a rolling pin, stretch the first ball of dough out to form a circle 25 cm (10 in) across. When it is about right, use your fingers to push the dough to the edges, forming a thick rim. Lay the dough on a well-floured, cold baking tray, or even a sheet of strong cardboard, as long as it is amply floured. Arrange half the potato slices over the pizza, leaving the rim bare. Lay half the anchovies randomly on top, then dot half the mascarpone around in teaspoonfuls. Season liberally, then drizzle a thin trickle of olive oil over the top. Repeat with the remaining dough and topping ingredients.

Open the oven and carefully shake and slide the pizzas onto the hot baking trays inside. Bake for 10–15 minutes, until the edges are lightly tanned and the potatoes are beginning to brown. Take out of the oven and quickly divide the rocket between the pizzas, piling it casually over the surface. Drizzle over a last shot of olive oil, grind a little pepper over the top and then serve, with the rocket just beginning to soften here and there in the heat.

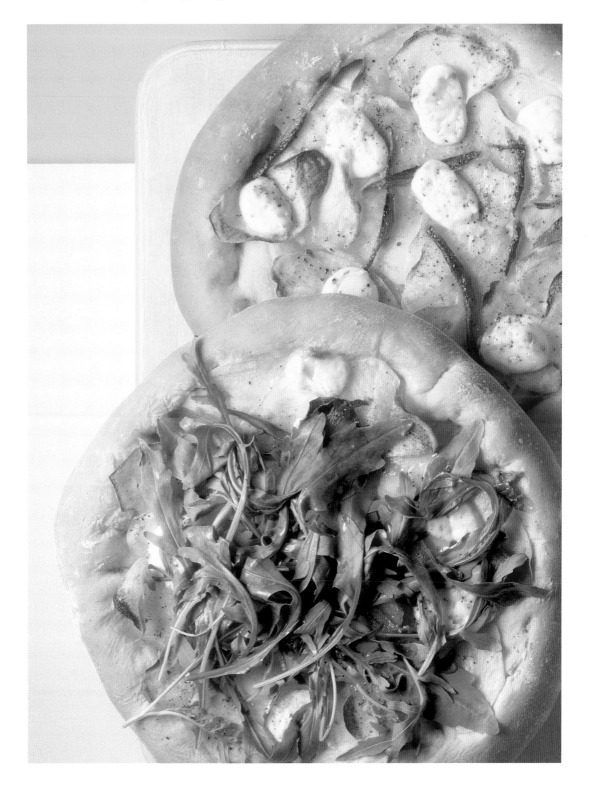

three-tomato tart with marjoram

Somehow this isn't quite a pizza, though it slides pretty close with its yeast dough and heavy complement of tomatoes. It is, in fact, constructed along the lines of a tart, with a bit more depth to it than a classic pizza. I like it just as it is, without any added cheese, but if you want a slight change, then try scattering a handful of Parmesan shavings (cut them from a block of Parmesan with a vegetable peeler) over the filling after it comes out of the oven. Either way it is delicious and substantial. I originally created it, minus cheese, for the vegan boyfriend of a very dear old friend. As it happens, he had given up on veganism by the time he got to try it, but no matter – we all loved it anyway.

SERVES 4

2½ TABLESPOONS SUN-DRIED TOMATO PURÉE OR RED PESTO

3 TABLESPOONS FINE CORNMEAL OR POLENTA

8 PLUM TOMATOES, SLICED

10 MEDIUM CHERRY TOMATOES, HALVED

½ TEASPOON THYME LEAVES

½ TEASPOON CASTER SUGAR

OLIVE OIL

A SMALL HANDFUL OF MARJORAM, OREGANO OR BASIL LEAVES

SALT AND FRESHLY GROUND BLACK PEPPER

FOR THE YEAST PASTRY:

225 G (8 OZ) STRONG WHITE FLOUR

115 G (4 OZ) PLAIN FLOUR

1 TEASPOON SALT

7 G SACHET OF EASY-BLEND YEAST

1 GENEROUS TABLESPOON OLIVE OIL

METHOD

To make the pastry, sift the two flours into a bowl with the salt and stir in the yeast. Make a well in the centre and add the olive oil and enough water to make a soft dough. Knead vigorously for 5–10 minutes, until satin-smooth and elastic. Place in an oiled bowl, turn to coat in oil, then cover with a damp tea towel and leave in a warm place to rise until doubled in bulk. If you want to slow its progress down (the tart is nicest served warm from the oven, not reheated), then pop it into the fridge.

Oil a 25 cm (10 in) tart tin. Punch the dough down and knead briefly, then spread the dough out thinly in the tin with your hands, pushing it up the sides. Spread the sun-dried tomato purée or red pesto over the base. Sprinkle 1½ tablespoons of the cornmeal evenly over the purée (this will sop up some of the juices from the fresh tomatoes). Now arrange the sliced plum tomatoes and halved cherry tomatoes, cut-side up, haphazardly over the tart, covering the base completely and thickly. Sprinkle with the remaining cornmeal plus the thyme leaves and sugar. Season with salt and plenty of pepper, then drizzle with 1½ tablespoons of olive oil. Let the tart sit for 10 minutes while the oven warms up.

Place a baking tray in the oven and heat to 230°C/450°F/Gas Mark 8. Pop the tart onto the hot baking tray and bake for 15 minutes, until the edges are puffed and golden brown. Brush the pastry with a little extra oil, then return to the oven for 5 minutes. Serve hot or warm, scattering over the fresh marjoram, oregano or basil just before taking the tart to the table.

himmel und erde

Himmel und Erde means 'heaven and earth', though the connotations here are not particularly spiritual. It refers to the two main ingredients: apples from up above (i.e. trees) and potatoes from the earth. The Germans are particularly strong on combinations of fruit with savoury ingredients, and this is a favourite of mine.

SERVES 4 GENEROUSLY

1 KG (2 LB 4 OZ) FLOURY POTATOES

450 G (1 LB) COOKING APPLES

SUGAR

A GENEROUS KNOB OF BUTTER

SALT AND FRESHLY GROUND BLACK PEPPER

METHOD

Peel the potatoes and cut into chunks. Put in a pan with just enough lightly salted water to cover them. Bring to the boil and simmer until almost cooked. Meanwhile, peel, core and roughly chop the apples.

Pour off about two-thirds of the water the potatoes are cooking in, then add the apples and simmer gently until they have collapsed and the potatoes are melting. Mash together, and season with salt, pepper and a little sugar. Stir in the butter, then tip into a serving dish and serve.

asparagus and gruyère quiche

This is a quiche to make at the height of the asparagus season when you've feasted your fill of plainly cooked asparagus. It is an excellent way of stretching a small quantity of asparagus.

SERVES 6–8

350 G (12 OZ) SHORTCRUST PASTRY (SEE PAGE 141)

350 G (12 OZ) ASPARAGUS

115G (4 OZ) GRUYÈRE CHEESE

3 SHALLOTS OR 1 SMALL ONION, CHOPPED

15 G (½ OZ) BUTTER

3 EGGS

150 ML (¼ PINT) MILK

90 ML (3 FL OZ) DOUBLE CREAM

1 TABLESPOON CHOPPED CHERVIL OR PARSLEY

SALT AND FRESHLY GROUND BLACK PEPPER

METHOD

Line a 23 cm (9 in) tart tin with the pastry. Leave it to rest in the fridge for 30 minutes. Pre-heat the oven to 200°C/400°F/Gas Mark 6.

Prick the base of the tart with a fork and line with greaseproof paper or foil and weigh down with baking beans. Bake for 10 minutes. Remove the paper or foil and beans and return to the oven for 5 minutes to dry out. Leave to cool. Reduce the oven temperature to 180°C/350°F/Gas Mark 4.

Trim the asparagus, breaking off the tough ends (save these and their cooking water for making soup). Cut into 2 cm (¾ in) lengths, keeping the tips separate.

Pour 4 cm (1½ in) of water into a large pan, add salt and bring to the boil. Add the stem pieces of asparagus and simmer for 5 minutes. Add the tips and simmer gently for 2–3 minutes, until almost *al dente*, but still firm. Drain. If prepared in advance, cool and cover.

Dice 85 g (3 oz) of the Gruyère, grating the remainder. Fry the shallots or onion gently in the butter until tender, without browning. Scatter the asparagus, diced Gruyère and shallots over the base of the pastry case.

Whisk the eggs lightly, then whisk in the milk, cream, chervil or parsley and salt and pepper. Pour over the asparagus and cheese. Scatter the grated Gruyère over the top and bake for 25–30 minutes, until just set in the centre and nicely browned. Serve hot, warm or cold.

fish gratin

This is a wickedly creamy, luxurious sort of gratin, the type one shouldn't eat too often, tempting though it is. The cream and egg yolks give the sauce a voluptuous texture, and the pungency of Parmesan sets if all off brilliantly. Shrimps or prawns may be optional, but I'd be loath to leave them out.

SERVES 4 GENEROUSLY

750 G (1 LB 8 OZ) WHITE FISH FILLETS (SUCH AS COD OR HADDOCK)

100 G (4 OZ) COOKED SHRIMPS OR PRAWNS (SHELLED WEIGHT), ROUGHLY
  CHOPPED (OPTIONAL)

1 TABLESPOON LEMON JUICE

45 G (1½ OZ) BUTTER

30 G (1 OZ) FLOUR

300 ML (½ PINT) MILK

150 ML (¼ PINT) SINGLE CREAM

2 EGG YOLKS

60 G (2 OZ) PARMESAN OR OTHER FULL-FLAVOURED HARD CHEESE,
  FRESHLY GRATED

SALT AND FRESHLY GROUND BLACK PEPPER

METHOD

Pre-heat the oven to 180°C/350°F/Gas Mark 4.

Put the fish fillets into a lightly buttered ovenproof dish and season with salt, pepper and lemon juice. Cover with foil and bake in the oven for about 20 minutes, until just cooked. Drain off any liquid and quickly flake the fish, discarding the skin. Place in a shallow gratin dish.

Meanwhile melt the butter in a saucepan and stir in the flour. Stir for a minute, then draw off the heat and gradually mix in the milk, a little at a time, followed by the cream. Simmer for 5-10 minutes, until thick, with no trace of raw flour taste. Draw off the heat again and stir in the shrimps or prawns (if using), then the egg yolks, salt and pepper. Pour over the cooked fish and sprinkle with Parmesan. Whip under a pre-heated grill until nicely browned.

If you've cooked the fish in advance, or are using left-overs from another meal, prepare as above, but finish the gratin in the oven at about 190°C/375°F/Gas Mark 5, baking until nicely browned – about 20–25 minutes.

sun-dried tomato bread

This recipe can also be made with tomato purée as a replacement for sun-dried tomatoes, and the tomato oil in the dough replaced with olive oil. After the dough has had its first rising, knead it for about 3 minutes, to smooth it out. Using the palms of your hands, flatten out the dough and then smear it thickly with the purée. Roll up like a Swiss roll and then settle it as neatly as you can in its tin. Bake as above.

MAKES A 450 G (1 LB) LOAF

450 G (1 LB) STRONG WHITE FLOUR

1½ TEASPOONS SALT

7 G SACHET OF EASY-BLEND YEAST

1 TEASPOON SUGAR

2 TABLESPOONS OLIVE OIL, FROM THE JAR OF TOMATOES

½ JAR SUN-DRIED TOMATOES IN OLIVE OIL, DRAINED AND CHOPPED

METHOD

Mix the flour with the salt, yeast and sugar. Add the olive oil and enough water to form a soft dough. It is better to err marginally on the damp side, as the flour absorbs a good deal of water during kneading. If the worst comes to the worst, dust overly sticky dough with extra flour as you knead.

Knead the bread energetically for a good 5 minutes, until it is satin-smooth and elastic. Return to the bowl and cover with a damp tea towel. Leave in a warm place until it has doubled in bulk, which will take around an hour, depending on the room temperature.

Punch the dough down, knead briefly and then spread it out as best you can. Dot with half the sun-dried tomatoes, roll up, knead again briefly and then repeat. Give it another quick kneading to distribute the pieces of sun-dried tomato evenly. Place in a greased 450 g (1 lb) loaf tin. Cover with a damp tea towel and again leave in a warm place until the dough has risen to fill the tin. Pre-heat the oven to 220°C/425°F/Gas Mark 7.

Bake the loaf for about 25–30 minutes, until it is cooked through. To test, turn the tin upside-down and shake the bread out – it should slide out fairly easily. Tap the bottom: if it sounds hollow, the bread is done. If the loaf sticks mercilessly to the tin, or all you get is a dull thud when you tap it, return to the oven for another 5 minutes or so to finish cooking. Leave the loaf to cool on a wire rack.

saffron teabread

If you've ever read anything about saffron, you are bound to know that it is the most expensive spice in the world, worth more than its weight in gold; but for its exalted past and honoured present, it is a spice that rewards the user tenfold. A tiny amount, a small fraction of a gram, betrays its presence in any dish with all the grandeur of true nobility, bestowing its pure golden colour streaked sparsely with fiery red and, naturally, its remarkable, incomparable flavour.

Describing the taste of saffron is well-nigh impossible. It's often labelled bitter-sweet. I think it has a surprisingly alluring, metallic edge to it, but the description I like best is 'honey laced with the sea'. This comes not from some romantic Eastern poet but from a commercial grower in north Wales, Caroline Riden, who is quite besotted with the stuff. She says, too, that using it is like cooking with living gold.

Though Caroline's range of saffron recipes spans all the great saffron countries, she particularly likes to use it in baking, an art that still thrives in Wales. This teabread is lifted instantly out of the ordinary by the addition of saffron. If you want to slice it neatly, you will have to keep it for a day to firm up, but I admit to loving it warm from the oven even if it does crumble hopelessly.

MAKES 1 LOAF

A GOOD PINCH OF SAFFRON STRANDS

100 G (3½ OZ) BUTTER

100 G (3½ OZ) CASTER SUGAR

100 G (3½ OZ) GOLDEN SULTANAS

60 G (2 OZ) GLACÉ CHERRIES, HALVED

250 G (9 OZ) PLAIN FLOUR

2 TEASPOONS BAKING POWDER

A PINCH OF SALT

METHOD

Put the saffron in a jar or jug and pour in 225 ml (8 fl oz) of hot water. Leave for 20 minutes (or longer if more convenient).

Put the butter and sugar into a pan large enough to take all the ingredients and stir over a moderate heat, until the butter has melted and mixed evenly with the sugar. Now add the sultanas and cherries, give them a quick stir and then pour in the saffron water, complete with all the threads. Return to the heat and simmer gently for 5 minutes. Leave to cool.

Pre-heat the oven to 180°C/350°F/Gas Mark 4. Prepare a 450 g (1 lb) loaf tin by greasing it and then cutting two wide strips of non-stick baking parchment and laying them at right angles to each other in the tin, pressing down and against the sides. One runs the length of the tin and overhangs each end, while the other sits over the first, running across the tin and overhanging the sides. The idea is to form a sort of cradle, so that the cooked loaf can just be lifted straight out of the tin when it is done.

Sift the flour with the baking powder and salt. Tip into the saffron mixture and stir to form a batter. Pour into the prepared loaf tin and smooth down. Bake for 1–1¼ hours, or until a skewer inserted into the centre comes out clean. Lift out of the tin on to a wire rack and leave to cool. Serve thickly sliced and plentifully buttered.

banana teabread

How many times have you thrown out the last few bananas because they've gone all brown and a bit squishy? And you must have seen past-their-prime bananas being sold off cheaply at the end of the day in markets and greengrocers'. Well, this is one excellent way to use up those sorry specimens of banana-hood, transforming them into a teatime bread that is gorgeous just sliced and buttered, and superb toasted for breakfast.

MAKES 1 LOAF

300 G (10 OZ) SELF-RAISING FLOUR

1 LEVEL TEASPOON BAKING POWDER

½ TEASPOON GROUND CINNAMON

¼ TEASPOON SALT

115 G (4 OZ) LIGHT MUSCOVADO SUGAR

300 G (10 OZ) PEELED BANANAS (ROUGHLY 3 LARGE ONES)

2 TEASPOONS LEMON JUICE

2 LARGE EGGS

1 TEASPOON VANILLA ESSENCE

175 ML (6 FL OZ) SUNFLOWER OIL

2 TABLESPOONS POPPY SEEDS

METHOD

Pre-heat the oven to 180°C/350°F/Gas Mark 4.

Sift the flour with the baking powder, cinnamon and salt, then stir in the sugar. Mash the bananas with the lemon juice and beat in the eggs, vanilla essence and oil. Add to the dry ingredients and mix well, then stir in the poppy seeds. Pour into a greased 450 g (1 lb) loaf tin and bake for 55–65 minutes, until well risen and browned. Poke a skewer into the centre – if it comes out clean, the teabread is done.

Turn out and leave to cool on a wire rack, then wrap in clingfilm or foil. Leave for at least 24 hours before eating. Serve sliced and buttered.

polenta syrup cake

This beautiful, burnished-gold cake, soaked in a sweet citrus syrup, is fairly quick to make and perfect for a tea party, since it needs to be baked a day in advance. It is at its best served with Greek yoghurt, to cut the sweetness, and soft fruit, in season.

SERVES 6-8

3 EGGS

110 G (4 OZ) CASTER SUGAR

110 G (4 OZ) BUTTER, MELTED AND COOLED UNTIL TEPID

JUICE OF ½ ORANGE

225 G (8 OZ) POLENTA OR FINE CORNMEAL

½ TABLESPOON BAKING POWDER

PINCH OF SALT

FINELY GRATED ZEST OF ½ LEMON

FINELY GRATED ZEST OF 1 ORANGE

1 TEASPOON VANILLA ESSENCE

GREEK YOGHURT, TO SERVE

SOFT FRUIT, IF IN SEASON, TO SERVE

FOR THE SYRUP:

JUICE OF 2 ORANGES

JUICE OF ½ LEMON

140 G (5 OZ) CASTER SUGAR

METHOD

Pre-heat the oven to 190°C/375°F/Gas Mark 5. Line a 20 cm (8 in) cake tin with non-stick baking parchment. Whisk the eggs with the caster sugar until pale and thick. Beat in the butter and the orange juice. Mix the polenta or cornmeal with the baking powder and salt and gradually beat it into the egg mixture. Stir in the two zests and the vanilla essence. Pour the cake batter into the prepared tin. Place in the oven and immediately reduce the heat to 170°C/325°F/Gas Mark 3. Bake for about 30-40 minutes, until the cake is brown and pulling away from the tin. Test it with a skewer, which should come out clean.

Once the cake is in the oven, make the syrup. Put all the ingredients into a pan and bring to the boil. Simmer gently for 5 minutes. Leave to cool.

When the cake comes out of the oven, make holes in it with a skewer and pour over the cool syrup. Leave to cool. Turn the cake out and serve with Greek yoghurt and soft fruits.

lavender shortbread

Nothing more than straight shortbread with some lavender flowers worked into the mixture. It adds a delicate lavender fragrance, turning good shortbread into something even better. To measure the lavender, first pick the little flowerlets off the stems. If you use dried lavender, use less as it has a stronger flavour.

MAKES 12 PETTICOAT TAILS

85 G (3 OZ) PLAIN FLOUR

85 G (3 OZ) CORNFLOUR

115 G (4 OZ) UNSALTED OR SLIGHTLY SALTED BUTTER, SOFTENED

60 G (2 OZ) CASTER SUGAR

3–3½ TEASPOONS FRESH LAVENDER FLOWERS OR 2–2½ TEASPOONS DRIED
LAVENDER FLOWERS

METHOD

Pre-heat the oven to 150°C/300°F/Gas Mark 2.

Sift the flour with the cornflour. Beat the butter with the sugar until light and creamy. Work in the flour and lavender to form a soft dough. Knead briefly to even out, then roll out (cover the dough with a sheet of greaseproof paper, then roll over that, so that the rolling pin doesn't stick) or press out with your hands on a baking tray, to form a circle about 5 mm (¼ in) thick. Prick all over with a fork, then bake for about 30 minutes, until a very pale biscuit colour. Remove from the oven and, while still warm, score the surface with a sharp knife to form 12 wedges (the petticoat tales). Leave to cool, then break along the scored lines. Store in an airtight tin.

sweet rice fritters

An alternative way to serve up your rice pudding, these fritters are crisp on the outside and creamy and tender inside. The starch in the risotto rice gives them extra richness and helps them to hold together, without being too heavy and doughy. Lovely as they are with no more than a sprinkling of sugar, they are even better with spoonfuls of home-made jam.

SERVES 4-6

115 G (4 OZ) RISOTTO RICE

500 ML (18 FL OZ) CREAMY MILK

A PINCH OF SALT

30 G (1 OZ) CASTER SUGAR

30 G (1 OZ) BUTTER

FINELY GRATED ZEST OF 1 LEMON

3 EGGS, SEPARATED

60 G (2 OZ) PLAIN FLOUR, SIFTED

2 TABLESPOONS COINTREAU OR GRAND MARNIER

SUNFLOWER OR OLIVE OIL, FOR FRYING

SUGAR OR, BLACKCURRANT OR RASPBERRY JAM, TO SERVE

METHOD

Put the rice, milk and salt in a large pan and simmer gently for 15 minutes.

Now add the sugar, butter and lemon zest. Continue cooking until the rice is very tender and has absorbed the milk. Draw off the heat and leave to cool. Beat in the egg yolks and then the sifted flour and liqueur. Shortly before frying, whisk the egg whites stiffly and fold them in.

Pour 1 cm (½ in) of oil into a frying pan and heat up over a medium heat. Drop in tablespoonfuls of the mixture, flatten slightly and fry on both sides, until golden brown. Drain briefly on kitchen paper and serve piping hot, dusted with extra sugar, or with a spoonful of blackcurrant or raspberry jam.

rice pudding brûlée

I have a bit of a thing about rice pudding and I'm not afraid to admit it. I love the stuff and always have. I even liked school rice pudding – and the prunes that came with it (but that's another story). Never fear, this is nothing like it. Under the crisp shell of caramelized sugar awaits an idyll of soft, tender grains in creamy cooked-down milk, with an elusive, almondy flavour that may puzzle the unknowing. It comes from a bay leaf, which was used to flavour milk puddings in this country for centuries, until we consigned it to the realms of the savoury. Try it and discover how unexpectedly good it can be.

Incidentally, these need to be made well in advance (in the morning for the evening, say) so that they have time to cool down twice over.

SERVES 2

300 ML (10 FL OZ) MILK

1 BAY LEAF, SNAPPED IN HALF

30 G (1 OZ) PUDDING RICE

1 TABLESPOON CASTER SUGAR

15 G (½ OZ) UNSALTED BUTTER

2 TABLESPOONS DEMERARA SUGAR

METHOD

Pour the milk into a pan and add the bay leaf. Bring slowly to the boil. Turn off the heat, cover and leave to infuse for 30 minutes. Remove the bay leaf and strain the milk on to the pudding rice in a second saucepan. Stir in the caster sugar, then bring up to the boil. Simmer gently for 20–30 minutes, stirring occasionally, until creamy. Grease two 150 ml (¼ pint) ramekins with the butter and pour in the rice mixture. Leave to cool.

Pre-heat the grill thoroughly. Sprinkle 1 tablespoon of demerara sugar over each ramekin and grill until the sugar melts and bubbles, which should take some 3–5 minutes. Leave to cool. As it cools, the sugar hardens to a solid crust. Serve the rice pudding brûlées either at room temperature or lightly chilled.

margaret pover's moist lemon cake

Mrs Pover, who runs an immaculate bed and breakfast between her bouts of cake-making, has made these lovely, syrupy, sharp lemon cakes so often that she can recite the recipe from memory, and no longer needs to look up quantities. In a matter of minutes, she whizzes up a new batch of batter and it's straight into the oven. Her cakes usually get eaten pretty swiftly, but if needs be, they will keep particularly well in an airtight container in a cool place.

SERVES 8

175 G (6 OZ) CASTER SUGAR

175 G (6 OZ) SELF-RAISING FLOUR

175 G (6 OZ) SOFTENED BUTTER

1 LEVEL TEASPOON BAKING POWDER

3 MEDIUM EGGS

FINELY GRATED ZEST OF 1 LARGE LEMON

75 ML (2½ FL OZ) MILK

TO FINISH:

3 TABLESPOONS GRANULATED SUGAR, PLUS A LITTLE EXTRA

JUICE OF 1 LARGE LEMON

A FEW CURLS OF LEMON ZEST

METHOD

Pre-heat the oven to 180°C/350°F/Gas Mark 4. Line the base of an 18–20 cm (7–8 in) cake tin with non-stick baking parchment and grease the sides.

Put all the ingredients for the cake into a food processor and process until smooth and evenly mixed, to produce a fairly runny cake batter. Pour into the prepared tin and bake for 40–50 minutes, until a skewer inserted in the centre comes out clean. Let the cake stand in the tin for 5 minutes, then turn out on to a plate. With a fine skewer pierce a dozen or so holes in the cake.

While the cake is in the oven, make the lemon syrup by stirring the 3 tablespoons of sugar into the lemon juice until dissolved. Pour this syrup over the cake once it has been turned out and pierced. Sprinkle the top with a thin, even layer of granulated sugar, then finish with a few curls of lemon zest scattered prettily over the top.

betty skelly's chocolate cake

Betty's cake is another quick and easy one to put together, yielding up a light, plain chocolate sponge of a traditional sort.

She likes to dust the plain butter icing with cocoa to give a dark finish and take the edge off the sweetness. My one suggestion would be to splash out on unrefined icing sugar, with its distinct pale tan colour and mild caramel flavour, which will give the icing an extra dimension.

SERVES 8 GENEROUSLY

140 G (5 OZ) SELF-RAISING FLOUR

30 G (1 OZ) COCOA POWDER

175 G (6 OZ) SOFTENED BUTTER

175 G (6 OZ) CASTER SUGAR

3 LARGE EGGS

FOR THE BUTTER ICING:

45 G (1½ OZ) SOFTENED BUTTER

140 G (5 OZ) ICING SUGAR

1 TABLESPOON COCOA POWDER, MIXED WITH 2 TEASPOONS HOT WATER

EXTRA COCOA POWDER, FOR DUSTING

METHOD

Pre-heat the oven to 180°C/350°F/Gas Mark 4. Line the base of an 18 cm (7 in) cake tin with non-stick baking parchment and grease the sides.

Sift the flour with the cocoa. Cream the butter and sugar together until light and fluffy. Beat in the eggs one at a time, adding a tablespoonful of flour with the last one. Fold in the remaining flour. Spoon into the cake tin and bake for 35–40 minutes, until a skewer inserted in the centre comes out clean. Leave in the tin for a few minutes, then turn out and leave to cool on a wire rack.

To make the butter icing, cream the butter with the icing sugar and the cocoa mixture until light and fluffy. Spread it over the top of the cake, then use a fork to make either little tufts and peaks or wavy lines in the icing. Dust lightly with a little extra cocoa powder before serving.

hungarian pancakes

Everyone loves pancakes in Hungary. Afternoon tea consists of endless pancakes, sweetened with home-made jams, or sugar and cinnamon. Pancakes also form the wrapping for more complicated fillings, both sweet and savoury.

A good pancake is thin and light and never flabby. It may take a few attempts to get it right, but pancake batter is fairly untemperamental and survives a bit of tampering with.

MAKES ABOUT 12

175 G (6 OZ) FLOUR

A PINCH OF SALT

1 TEASPOON SUGAR

3 EGGS

225 ML (8 FL OZ) MILK

225 ML (8 FL OZ) FIZZY MINERAL WATER

BUTTER, FOR COOKING

METHOD

Sift the flour with the salt and add the sugar. Make a well in the centre and break in the eggs. Add about half the milk. Stir gradually, drawing in the flour and adding the remaining milk slowly, to form a smooth batter. Leave to rest for 30 minutes. Just before using, stir in enough of the mineral water to make a thin batter with the consistency of runny single cream.

While the batter is resting, clarify the butter – this rids it of impurities and makes it less likely to burn. Heat it gently in a saucepan, skimming off any scum that rises to the surface. Leave to stand off the heat for a few minutes, until the white sediment has settled at the bottom. Carefully pour off the clarified butter, leaving the sediment behind.

Brush a heavy pan, about 20–23 cm (8–9 in) in diameter, with clarified butter and heat thoroughly. Stir the batter. Pour a small ladleful of batter into the pan, then tip and tilt it so that the batter covers the base. Pour out any excess. As soon as the batter has set and bubbles begin to show on the upper surface, turn the pancake over and cook for a few more seconds until lightly browned underneath. Continue, brushing the pan with butter between pancakes, until all the batter is used up.

The first pancake nearly always sticks, so think of it purely as a tester (and cook's perk). If it is rather thick, thin down the batter with a little extra mineral water. Pile up the pancakes as you cook and keep them warm if you are using them immediately. Serve sweet with jam, or sugar and cinnamon, or sugar and lemon juice.

If you are making the pancakes in advance, or want to freeze them, lay a strip of greaseproof paper between each pair. When cool, wrap neatly in cling film.

violet graham's scones

In the village of Marwood in Devon, Violet Graham is acknowledged queen of the light-as-air scone. For a gentle sheen, brush the tops with a little milk before baking. Serve the scones warm from the oven, with clotted cream and strawberry jam or, failing that, whipped cream or butter and any good jam.

MAKES 20 SMALL SCONES

2 LARGE EGGS

MILK

450 G (1 LB) SELF-RAISING FLOUR

2 TEASPOONS BAKING POWDER

115 G (4 OZ) BUTTER, DICED

60 G (2 OZ) CASTER SUGAR

METHOD

Pre-heat the oven to 220°C/425°F/Gas Mark 7.

Beat the eggs together lightly in a measuring jug, then add enough milk to make up to 300 ml (10 fl oz) and whisk together lightly. Sift the flour with the baking powder. Rub in the butter until the mixture resembles fine breadcrumbs. Stir in the sugar, then stir in enough of the egg and milk mixture to give a soft but not sticky dough – you may not need it all.

Turn out on to a lightly floured work surface and knead lightly. Roll out to a thickness of 1 cm (½ in) and stamp out 5-cm (2-in) rounds. Place on greased baking trays and bake for about 10 minutes, until pale golden brown.

fig jam

This jam was inspired by the breakfast jams of Mme Manet at the Hôtel des Trois Lys in Condom. A brush with Weight Watchers induced her to reduce the sugar content of her home-made jams, and they taste all the better for it. However, less sugar means that this jam won't reach a firm set, always remaining more runny than the usual British style of jam.

MAKES ABOUT 1.5 KG (3 LB 5 OZ)

900 G (2 LB) PURPLE OR GREEN FIGS, NOT TOO RIPE

2 LEMONS

3 CLOVES

450 G (1 LB) GRANULATED OR CASTER SUGAR

METHOD

Nip the hard stems off the figs, then quarter the fruit. Grate the zest of the lemons finely. Squeeze the juice and reserve the pips. Tie the pips and the cloves in a square of muslin. Put the figs in a pan with the lemon juice, muslin bag and 150 ml (5 fl oz) of water. Heat gently and simmer for 15 minutes until the figs are tender. Now add the sugar and lemon zest and stir until the sugar has completely dissolved. Bring back to the boil and boil until thick and syrupy – about 40 minutes.

Remove the muslin bag and let the jam settle for 5 minutes. Ladle into hot sterilized jam jars (see tip on page 6), cover and seal as normal. Store in a cool dark place and use within 3 months. Store the jars, once opened, in the fridge.

5 picnics

seared chicken and peach sandwich with basil mayo ■ **pan bagnat** ■ three suns **sandwich** ■ **grilled aubergine sandwich** with mascarpone and sun-dried tomatoes ■ **devilled drumsticks** ■ **arancini** ■ pea, ricotta and herb **quiche** ■ sage and sunflower seed **rolls** ■ oded schwartz's **carrot and almond chutney** ■ **falafel** ■ hildegard's potato and beetroot **salad** ■ broad bean, oven-dried tomato and bacon **salad** ■ kumar's **sri lankan carrot salad** ■ **couscous** with roast tomatoes, peppers and goats' cheese ■ fresh hyssop and cornmeal **focaccia** ■ **rice salad** with apricots ■ chorizo and egg **bread**

seared chicken and peach sandwich with basil mayo

I've got to admit that I was particularly pleased with this big sandwich. Griddling the peaches brings out their full fragrance, and the warmth of the chicken and the peaches together persuades the basil in the mayonnaise to put on its very best, most aromatic show. Chicken thighs are very cheap, especially if you buy them with the bone in and remove it yourself (just cut down through the flesh along the length of the bone, then use a small, sharp, flexible knife to cut the flesh away from the bone, carefully working your way around it). They also have much more flavour than the more expensive breast meat. Make the most of it!

SERVES 2

2 CHICKEN THIGHS, BONED (BUT NOT SKINNED)

JUICE OF ½ LEMON

2-3 TABLESPOONS OLIVE OIL

1 CIABATTA LOAF OR BAGUETTE

1 PEACH, HALVED AND STONED

A FEW LEAVES OF COS LETTUCE

SALT AND FRESHLY GROUND BLACK PEPPER

FOR THE MAYONNAISE:

A SMALL HANDFUL OF BASIL LEAVES

A PINCH OF SUGAR

A PINCH OF SALT

2-3 TABLESPOONS MAYONNAISE

METHOD

Marinate the chicken thighs in the lemon juice, olive oil, salt and pepper for at least an hour.

To make the mayonnaise, pound the basil, sugar and salt to a rough paste in a mortar, then work in the mayonnaise. Taste and adjust the seasoning.

When you are beginning to get peckish, halve the bread lengthways, then wrap it in foil and heat through in a gentle oven. Oil a griddle pan and set over a strong heat (or heat up the grill and line the grill pan with foil). Leave to heat up for 3 or 4 minutes at least. Shake excess marinade off the chicken and lay it on the griddle (or under the grill, close to the heat at first). Leave undisturbed for 3 minutes and don't worry about the smoke. Turn and repeat on the other side. Meanwhile, brush the peach with oil and lay it on the griddle. Leave for about 3 minutes, then turn and leave for another 3 minutes. Reduce the heat under the griddle so that the chicken can cook through without burning to smithereens – it'll need another 3 or 4 minutes or so, turning it once or twice.

When the chicken and peaches are nearly done, start assembling the sandwich. Slather both sides of the inside of the bread with the basil mayonnaise. Line the bottom half with lettuce leaves. As soon as the chicken is done, slice each piece diagonally to form large wedges. Slice the peaches roughly too, then load the bread with chicken and peach. Clamp on the top, cut in half and tuck in.

pan bagnat

In Provence, pan bagnat, is made with a long white loaf, usually one that is a little broader than a baguette. Find a loaf with a sturdy, crisp crust and plenty of flavour and character, which also happens to be relatively flat. No more than 10 cm (4 in) in height. I find that a plain or olive ciabatta is the best bet.

Pan Bagnat is that rare thing, a sandwich that positively benefits from being made in advance (up to about 12 hours), so don't leave it until the last minute.

SERVES 2-4

GOOD BREAD (SEE ABOVE), OR EXCELLENT, CHEWY, LARGE ROLLS

GARLIC CLOVES, CRUSHED

RED WINE VINEGAR

EXTRA VIRGIN OIL

EXCELLENT TOMATOES

FRESH BASIL LEAVES

SALT AND FRESHLY GROUND BLACK PEPPER

SUGAR, IF NECESSARY

FOR THE FILLING (ANY OR ALL OF THE FOLLOWING, AS THE FANCY TAKES YOU):

CRISP LETTUCE, SHREDDED

SLICES OF SALAMI, SKINNED

BLACK OLIVES, STONED

TINNED OR MARINATED ANCHOVY FILLETS

HARD-BOILED EGGS, SHELLED AND SLICED OR QUARTERED

CAPERS

TAPENADE (SEE PAGE 142)

TINNED TUNA, DRAINED AND FLAKED

PEPPERS, GRILLED AND SKINNED

SPRING ONIONS, SLICED

RED ONION, THINLY SLICED

RADISHES, SLICED

METHOD

Cut the loaf in half horizontally. Pull out a little of the insides to make a cavity on both, to hold the filling. Rub what is left with the cut side of a garlic clove. Make a quick vinaigrette (see page 141). Drizzle a little over both sides.

Begin to build up the layers of filling. Start with tomatoes, which are absolutely essential. Make a bed of tomatoes on the base, season with a pinch of sugar, then scatter over the basil. After that, start to pile in whichever of the other ingredients you fancy. Pack the filling until it bulges high above the bread. Drizzle a little vinaigrette over the ingredients every now and then, so that they are nicely seasoned but not swimming in dressing.

Place the top of the loaf over the filling and press down firmly. Wrap tightly in cling film and place weights on top. Leave for at least 1½ hours to compact.

To serve, cut into large chunks or wedges, and provide plenty of napkins to wipe messy chins and fingers.

three suns sandwich

Here we have Italy meets France meets Spain all in one sandwich, and a big, picnic-worthy one at that. We start with an idea from the south of France – the *pan bagnat*, a stuffed loaf of a sandwich, compressed overnight so that dressing and juices ooze invitingly into the crumb of the bread (see page 104). For the bread I've chosen the lovely, chewy, open-crumbed Italian ciabatta, and for the filling I've headed to Spain with Manchego cheese and sherry vinegar. And there's more – olives and olive oil from whichever hot weather country you fancy, and air-dried ham from Italy, Spain or Portugal or, indeed, Britain, if you want to anchor your flights of fantasy on home territory.

SERVES 3-4

1 CIABATTA LOAF, SPLIT IN HALF LENGTHWAYS

4-6 SLICES OF AIR-DRIED HAM, SUCH AS PARMA, SAN DANIELE,
    JAMÓN SERRANO, OR CUMBERLAND

85 G (3 OZ) MANCHEGO CHEESE, THINLY SLICED

2 RIPE TOMATOES, THINLY SLICED

A HANDFUL OF FRISÉE LETTUCE LEAVES

FOR THE DRESSING:

1 TABLESPOON SHERRY VINEGAR

7 TABLESPOONS OLIVE OIL

60 G (2 OZ) BLACK OR GREEN OLIVES, PITTED

1 FRESH RED CHILLI, SEEDED AND ROUGHLY CHOPPED

1 LEVEL TEASPOON CHOPPED OREGANO

2 TABLESPOONS CHOPPED PARSLEY

1 TABLESPOON CAPERS

2 CORNICHONS (BABY GHERKINS) OR 1 SMALL PICKLED
    GHERKIN, ROUGHLY CHOPPED

1-2 GARLIC CLOVES, CHOPPED

SALT AND FRESHLY GROUND BLACK PEPPER

METHOD

Begin with the dressing. Put all the ingredients into a food processor and process until finely mixed and chopped, adding a little more oil or vinegar, if necessary. If you don't have a processor, chop all the solid ingredients together very, very finely and then mix them with the oil and vinegar and season with salt and pepper.

Drizzle a few spoonfuls of the dressing over both the cut sides of the ciabatta. Now build up layers of ham, cheese, tomato and frisée on one half, anointing each layer with a little more of the dressing and season with pepper. Finally, clamp on the second half of the loaf and press down firmly. Wrap tightly in clingfilm, then lay on a board or plate and weight down with heavy weights (bags of dried beans, tins of tomatoes or whatever else is to hand). Leave overnight in the fridge. Unwrap and cut into chunks just before eating.

grilled aubergine sandwich
with mascarpone and sun-dried tomatoes

We filmed the titles for the television series *Taste of the Times* one chilly November day, popping in and out of shops and calling at food stalls along the length of London's Portobello Road and the adjoining Goldborne Road (a Mecca for anyone who likes Moroccan or Portuguese food). At lunchtime, we found ourselves under the flyover, where the best of the market ends, and dived into the Portobello Café for a quick lunch. The grilled aubergine sandwich with mascarpone and sun-dried tomatoes, sluiced down by a big mug of very British tea, was exactly what I needed to get me through the rest of the day.

SERVES 1

2 SLICES OF AUBERGINE, CUT ABOUT 2 CM (¾ IN) THICK,
   FROM STALK TO STEM END

OLIVE OIL

2 GENEROUS TABLESPOONS MASCARPONE

⅓–½ CIABATTA LOAF, SPLIT IN HALF AND WARMED THROUGH IN THE OVEN,
   OR 2 LARGE SLICES OF STURDY *PAIN DE CAMPAGNE*
   OR SOURDOUGH BREAD, LIGHTLY TOASTED

4 HALVES OF SUN-DRIED TOMATO, CUT INTO STRIPS

SALT AND LOTS OF FRESHLY GROUND BLACK PEPPER

METHOD

If you have time, salt the slices of aubergine lightly and leave for 30–60 minutes to degorge. Wipe dry, then brush with olive oil and grill under a thoroughly pre-heated grill, fairly close to the heat, until browned on both sides and tender through and through. Leave to cool until tepid. Spread the mascarpone on the cut sides of the ciabatta, or on each slice of bread. Season with salt and pepper. Sandwich the aubergine and the sun-dried tomatoes between the pieces of bread. Eat quickly, while still warm.

devilled drumsticks

The word 'devilled' brings enticing notions of wickedness to any dish, so I hope you won't be too disappointed when you realize that this is just a recipe for drumsticks baked in the oven in a sweet, sticky marinade. These days, this might more commonly be thought of as a barbecue sauce, but the old-fashioned English sense, referring to the spice of the Worcestershire sauce and the mustard, is much more vivid. In winter, serve the devilled drumsticks hot from the oven, but when summer comes they make good picnic fare, eaten cold, or can be cooked on the barbecue, as long as they are frequently brushed with the marinade as they sizzle in the heat.

SERVES 4

8 CHICKEN DRUMSTICKS

FOR THE MARINADE:

1 TABLESPOON WORCESTERSHIRE SAUCE

2 TABLESPOONS TOMATO KETCHUP

2 TABLESPOONS DARK MUSCOVADO SUGAR

1 TABLESPOON DARK SOY SAUCE

3 GARLIC CLOVES, CRUSHED

1 TABLESPOON DIJON OR ENGLISH MUSTARD

½ TABLESPOON RED OR WHITE WINE VINEGAR

1 TABLESPOON SUNFLOWER OIL

METHOD

Mix together all the marinade ingredients. Arrange the drumsticks in a single layer in a shallow ovenproof dish and pour over the marinade. Turn the drumsticks to coat, then cover and leave to marinate for at least 30 minutes, longer if you can – up to 24 hours in the fridge. If the chicken has been in the fridge, though, let it come back to room temperature before cooking.

Pre-heat the oven to 200°C/400°F/Gas Mark 6.

Spoon the marinade over the drumsticks one more time so that they are moist and evenly sozzled in it. Place the dish, drumsticks, marinade and all (uncovered), in the oven and bake for about 50 minutes, turning and basting the thighs roughly every 15 minutes so that they are browned and sticky all over. They can now be eaten hot from the oven, or left to cool in their juices and reheated thoroughly later, or eaten at room temperature.

arancini

Arancini, which literally means 'little oranges', are fried stuffed rice balls, and have long been one of my favourite snacks when I'm in the south of Italy. You can always get them at railway station buffets, and often at cafés. They are a little fiddly to make at home, but worth it in my book. Although they taste best when hot, they're not at all bad cold – just the thing for a picnic or packed lunch.

MAKES 12

350 G (12 OZ) RISOTTO RICE, SUCH AS ARBORIO

4 EGGS

85 G (3 OZ) CACIOCAVALLO OR PARMESAN CHEESE, FRESHLY GRATED

30 G (1 OZ) BUTTER

GROUND NUTMEG

5 TABLESPOONS VERY THICK TOMATO SAUCE (SEE PAGE 141)

60 G (2 OZ) GREEN PEAS (SHELLED WEIGHT), COOKED

60 G (2 OZ) MOZZARELLA CHEESE, CUBED

FLOUR

85 G (3 OZ) FINE DRY BREADCRUMBS

SUNFLOWER OR VEGETABLE OIL, FOR DEEP-FRYING

SALT AND FRESHLY GROUND BLACK PEPPER

METHOD

Cook the rice in plenty of boiling salted water until tender. Drain thoroughly. Mix with 2 of the eggs, the Caciocavallo or Parmesan cheese, the butter, nutmeg, salt and pepper. Work well with your hands until the mixture holds together, then leave to cool. Meanwhile simmer the tomato sauce and peas together for 5 minutes, then leave to cool.

Working on one at a time, divide the rice into 12 portions and roll into balls (wet your hands first to prevent sticking). Make a fairly capacious hole in the centre with your finger and insert a teaspoonful of the tomato/pea mixture and a cube of Mozzarella. Carefully cover the filling with a knob of rice, sealing it in completely. Mould back into a ball.

Beat the remaining eggs lightly. Roll the *Arancini* first in flour, then dip into beaten egg, shaking off the excess, and finally roll in breadcrumbs, making sure that each one is thoroughly and evenly coated. Deep-fry a few balls at a time in plenty of oil, pre-heated to about 160°C/325°F/Gas Mark 3, until richly browned. Drain on kitchen paper. Serve hot or warm.

To reheat, either pop back into the oil for a few minutes or heat through, uncovered, in a warm oven.

pea, ricotta and herb quiche

This is an enchantingly pretty, countryish quiche, with a puffed yeast dough crust filled with herb-flecked ricotta and peas. I think the yeast pastry is what makes it extra special, but if you are pushed for time, line the tart tin with shortcrust pastry and bake blind before filling. Use a mixture of at least three sweet, fresh herbs, such as parsley, chives, chervil, basil or marjoram. Thyme, lovage or salad burnet are good too, but use in small quantities as they are strongly flavoured. Like most quiches, this one is nicest when served warm.

SERVES 6-8

225 G (8 OZ) RICOTTA CHEESE

2 EGGS

200 ML (7 FL OZ) MILK

4 TABLESPOONS FRESHLY GRATED PARMESAN CHEESE

4 SPRING ONIONS, THINLY SLICED

3 TABLESPOONS CHOPPED MIXED SWEET HERBS (SUCH AS PARSLEY, CHIVES, CHERVIL, BASIL, MARJORAM, OREGANO, THYME, LOVAGE, SALAD BURNET)

350 G (12 OZ) COOKED PEAS

SALT AND FRESHLY GROUND BLACK PEPPER

FOR THE PASTRY:

200 G (7 OZ) STRONG WHITE FLOUR

SALT

½ SACHET OF EASY-BLEND YEAST

1 EGG

3 TABLESPOONS OLIVE OIL

METHOD

First make the pastry. Sift the flour with the salt. Stir in the yeast. Make a well in the centre and break in the egg. Add the oil. Gradually work into the flour, adding enough water to form a soft dough. Gather the dough up into a ball, knead for 5–10 minutes until smooth and elastic, set in a clean bowl, cover and leave to rise in a warm place until it has doubled in bulk.

While it rises, prepare the filling. Beat the ricotta with the eggs, and gradually mix in the milk. Stir in 3 tablespoons of the Parmesan, and all the spring onions, herbs, salt and pepper.

Place an upturned baking tray in the oven and heat to 190°C/375°F/Gas Mark 5. Punch down the dough and knead again briefly. Using the heel of your hand, press the dough into an oiled 25 cm (10 in) tart tin, easing the dough to cover the base and come up around the sides. The dough should be thickest around the sides, rising up a little above the rim of the tin.

Scatter the peas evenly over the dough. Stir the ricotta custard and pour over the peas. Sprinkle the remaining tablespoon of Parmesan over the surface. Set on the hot baking tray in the oven (which gives the base of the tart an instant blast of heat) and bake for 30–35 minutes, until barely set and golden. Serve hot, warm or cold.

sage and sunflower seed rolls

These rolls are heaven-sent for a fine slice of Cheddar or other good British hard cheese, though they are also irresistible warm from the oven, with nothing more than a smear of butter. Guard them jealously if you are making them for a special occasion, as they disappear in the twinkling of an eye in our household.

MAKES 6 ROLLS

15 G (½ OZ) FRESH YEAST

1 TEASPOON SUGAR

450 G (1 LB) STRONG WHITE FLOUR

1½ TEASPOONS SALT

1 TABLESPOON OLIVE OIL

30 G (1 OZ) SUNFLOWER SEEDS

2 TABLESPOONS CHOPPED SAGE

MILK, FOR BRUSHING

METHOD

Cream the yeast with 150 ml (¼ pint) of warm water and the sugar and leave in a warm place for 5–10 minutes, until it's frothing merrily. Sift the flour with the salt into a large bowl and make a well in the middle. Pour in the yeast mixture and the oil and start mixing, gradually adding more warm water, until you have a soft dough. Knead thoroughly for a good 5 minutes, until the dough is smooth and elastic. Place in a lightly oiled bowl, turn to coat in oil, then cover with a damp tea towel and leave in a warm place until it has doubled in bulk – about an hour.

Punch the dough down and gradually knead in the sunflower seeds and sage. Divide into 6 pieces and roll each one into a ball. Place the balls on a greased baking tray, flattening them slightly to give neat bun shapes. Leave plenty of space between the balls to allow them to expand. Leave in a warm place for about 30 minutes, until they have doubled in size. Pre-heat the oven to 200°C/400°F/Gas Mark 6.

Brush lightly with a little milk and bake for 20 minutes, until lightly browned. If they are done, the buns will lift easily off the tray. One final check – tap the underneath of one of the buns. If it sounds hollow, it really is done. Transfer to a wire rack to cool.

oded schwartz's
carrot and almond chutney

When Oded Schwartz sent us a jar of this irresistible chutney we simply couldn't stop eating it. The jar was passed around and around, with everyone dipping in, until it was all gone. Chutney or *chatni*, as it is known in Hindi, originated in India, but Oded's chutney is derived from various recipes, including carrot *halwa*, an Indian sweet, and a similar Jewish confection served at Passover. Oded recommends serving it with lamb, or hard, mature cheese. I like it so much I'm perfectly happy to eat it neat.

MAKES ABOUT 2.25 KG (5 LB)

900 G (2 LB) CARROTS

150 G (5 OZ) PEELED FRESH ROOT GINGER

FINELY GRATED ZEST AND JUICE
   OF 2 LEMONS

A PINCH OF GROUND CHILLI OR TO TASTE

30 G (1 OZ) SALT

30 G (1 OZ) GROUND CORIANDER

500 ML (18 FL OZ) CIDER VINEGAR

125 ML (4 FL OZ) CLEAR HONEY

675 G (1 LB 8 OZ) SUGAR

60 G (2 OZ) FLAKED ALMONDS

METHOD

Grate the carrots coarsely lengthways to achieve the longest possible strands. Cut half the ginger into matchsticks and grate the remainder finely. Mix the carrots and all the ginger with the lemon zest and juice, chilli, salt and coriander. Cover with the vinegar and leave overnight.

Transfer the marinated carrots and their juices to a preserving pan and add 300 ml (10 fl oz) of water. Bring to the boil and simmer for 20 minutes. Add the honey and sugar and stir to dissolve.

Bring back to the boil and boil for 25 minutes or until the mixture is thick. Stir in the almonds and boil for a further 4–5 minutes. Spoon into hot sterilized jars (see page 6) and seal immediately. The chutney can be eaten straight away, although it will improve after storing for a few months.

falafel

Falafel are deep-fried balls of ground chickpeas flavoured with garlic and parsley. They should be crisp on the outside, soft on the inside. Piled hot from frying into a warm pitta bread, with simple fresh salad and oodles of tahina dressing to smooth the whole lot together, they are quite sensational.

SERVES 4–8, DEPENDING ON HUNGER AND GREED

8 PITTA BREAD

4 TOMATOES, SEEDED AND ROUGHLY CHOPPED

½ CUCUMBER, PEELED AND DICED

6 COS OR OTHER FIRM LETTUCE LEAVES, SHREDDED

FOR THE TAHINA DRESSING:

175 G (6 OZ) LIGHT TAHINA PASTE

3 GARLIC CLOVES, CRUSHED

JUICE OF 1½–2 LEMONS

FOR THE FALAFEL:

225 G (8 OZ) CHICKPEAS, SOAKED FOR 24 HOURS

1 TABLESPOON CUMIN SEEDS

2 TEASPOONS CORIANDER SEEDS

1 SMALL ONION, CHOPPED

2 GARLIC CLOVES, CHOPPED

3 HEAPED TABLESPOONS CHOPPED FRESH CORIANDER

1 TABLESPOON FLOUR

¼ TEASPOON BAKING POWDER

SUNFLOWER OIL, FOR DEEP-FRYING

SALT AND FRESHLY GROUND BLACK PEPPER

METHOD

To make the falafel, begin by draining the chickpeas and tipping them into the bowl of a processor. Dry-fry the cumin and coriander seeds in a small, heavy frying pan over a high heat until they turn a little darker and their scent wafts through the kitchen. Cool and grind to a fine powder. Add to the chickpeas, together with the onion, garlic, fresh coriander, flour, baking powder, salt and pepper. Process together until smooth. To test for seasoning, break off a small knob of the mixture and shallow fry in a little oil. Taste and add more spices or salt if needed. Wet your hands and roll the remaining mixture into small balls – no bigger than a walnut, and even smaller for a higher ratio of crisp exterior to soft interior. Set aside until you are ready to fry them.

To make the tahina dressing, put the tahina paste into a bowl with the crushed garlic and lemon juice. Start to mix, gradually beating in enough water to make a creamy mixture with the consistency of double cream (90–150 ml or 3–5 fl oz should be about right). Don't worry that the tahina seizes up like cement at first. Keep adding water and beating and it will smooth out. Season with salt, and add a little more lemon juice if needed. Cover and set aside.

Put the pitta in a low oven to warm through and place the tomatoes, cucumber and lettuce in individual bowls on the table so that everyone can help themselves. Heat up a panful of sunflower oil (I actually use my wok for most deep-frying) over a moderate heat, until a small cube of bread dropped into the oil sizzles immediately, but doesn't start to brown straight away. Fry the falafel a few at a time, taking care not to overcrowd the pan. When they are richly browned (they should take about 8 minutes – any quicker and the interior won't be properly cooked), drain briefly on kitchen paper. Season with a little salt and take to the table for everyone to start making up their pittas, while you cook the remaining falafel.

The rough order to fill pitta breads is this: slit open the pitta bread along one of the long curved sides and put in a little of the diced tomato and maybe a shred or three of lettuce. Now drop in four or five falafel, then drizzle over some tahina. Add some more tomato and cucumber, stuff in more lettuce and finish with more tahina dressing if you can!

hildegard's potato and beetroot salad

This salad disapeared in the twinkling of an eye in our kitchen. In fact, it produced a scene of unabashed and embarrassing gluttony, forks flailing, all of us jostling to regain our positions near the bowl. The recipe comes from the mother of my friend Michele. Hildegard serves it at Christmas alongside the cold turkey and ham, but don't wait until then, it's ideal for picnics too.

SERVES 4-6

675 G (1 LB 8 OZ) POTATOES

1 MEDIUM-LARGE BEETROOT

250 G (9 OZ) *MATJES* OR DILL-PICKLED HERRINGS

½ ONION, FINELY CHOPPED

4 BABY GHERKINS, FINELY CHOPPED, OR 2 TABLESPOONS CAPERS, ROUGHLY CHOPPED

2 HARD-BOILED EGGS, SHELLED AND CHOPPED (OPTIONAL)

2-3 GENEROUS TABLESPOONS MAYONNAISE

SALT AND FRESHLY GROUND BLACK PEPPER

Cook the potatoes and beetroot separately. When cool enough to handle, peel both of them.

Cut the potatoes and beetroot into 1.5–2 cm (⅝–¾ in) cubes. Cut the herrings into strips about 2 cm (¾ in) long by 5 mm (¼ in) wide. Put them all into a bowl, with the onion, baby gherkins or capers and eggs, if using. Add enough mayonnaise to coat everything lightly and season with salt and pepper.

broad bean, oven-dried tomato and bacon salad

This salad is best served warm straight from the pan so that you can savour the flavours and enjoy the colours at their most vivid. It's worth taking a little trouble over broad beans, especially late in their season. Although the price is often very low, they can be on the large, tough side. It may seem a bit of a chore to skin each individual bean, but it pays dividends in terms of taste.

Oven-dried tomatoes are not the same as sun-dried tomatoes, I like to cook them slowly until they are semi-dried but still slightly fleshy. Halve the tomatoes across the equator and deseed carefully. Season with salt and leave upside down on a rack to drain for 30 minutes. Place cut-side up on a tray lined with non-stick baking parchment and bake for about 1½–2 hours at 160°C/325°F/Gas Mark 3. Check regularly towards the end of the cooking time. They should be frizzled round the edges but softly leathery in the centre.

If you don't want to use them immediately, you can preserve them by packing them into a clean, dry jar, adding a few cloves of garlic, a sprig of thyme or rosemary and maybe a dried chilli or two. Add enough olive oil to cover completely. Then store, tightly sealed, in the fridge.

SERVES 2

650 G (1 LB 7 OZ) FRESH BROAD BEANS IN THEIR PODS,
  OR 175-225 G (6-8 OZ) FROZEN BROAD BEANS, THAWED
1 THICK RASHER OF STREAKY BACON, RIND REMOVED,
  CUT INTO NARROW STRIPS
1 TABLESPOON OLIVE OR SUNFLOWER OIL
½ RED ONION, THINLY SLICED
1 GARLIC CLOVE, CHOPPED
1 OR 2 OVEN-DRIED TOMATOES, CUT INTO STRIPS
½ TABLESPOON RED WINE VINEGAR
½ TEASPOON DIJON MUSTARD
¼ TEASPOON SUGAR
SALT AND FRESHLY GROUND BLACK PEPPER

METHOD

Pod the broad beans if fresh. Blanch in boiling water for 1 minute, then drain. Using a sharp knife, make a slit in the end of each one and pop out the little bright-green beanlet inside. If using frozen broad beans, just let them thaw, then skin in the same way. Finish cooking the beans in fresh water for about 1–2 minutes for frozen, 2–3 minutes for fresh. Drain thoroughly.

Fry the bacon in the oil until lightly browned. Add the beans, onion and garlic and fry for a couple of minutes to heat through and to begin to soften the onion. The idea is that it should retain some of its freshness but have the edge taken off by the heat. Draw off the heat, allow to cool for a minute or so, stir in the sun-dried tomatoes, if using, then add the vinegar, mustard, sugar, salt and pepper. Stir to mix evenly and serve hot or warm.

kumar's sri lankan carrot salad

Kumar Vasanthakumar and his wife Harriet Festing were our hosts when we visited the small rural town of Wye. Here, in quaint rural Kent is a melting pot of people of all nationalities. Some come to study at the college for a few years, then return to their native countries, while others like Kumar, originally from Sri Lanka, stay on, settling down to throw their own special qualities and culture into the pot.

Kumar and I joined forces to cook supper together one evening and this is one of the deliciously spice-laden dishes he created for us.

Though these aromatic carrots are also superb hot, Kumar often serves them cold as a salad.

SERVES 4-6

1 LARGE ONION, CHOPPED

2 TABLESPOONS SUNFLOWER OIL

¼ TEASPOON BLACK MUSTARD SEEDS

½ TEASPOON CUMIN SEEDS

A PINCH OF FENUGREEK SEEDS

A HANDFUL OF CURRY LEAVES (OPTIONAL)

A SMALL PIECE OF PANDANUS LEAF (OPTIONAL)

2-3 GREEN CHILLIES, QUARTERED LENGTHWAYS AND SEEDED

SALT

450 G (1 LB) CARROTS, CUT INTO BATONS 5 CM (2 IN) LONG

½ TEASPOON GROUND TURMERIC

300 ML (½ PINT) COCONUT MILK

METHOD

Fry the onion in the oil for about 3 minutes, then add the mustard, cumin and fenugreek seeds, the curry leaves and pandanus leaf, if using, green chillies and salt and continue cooking until the onion is golden. Add the carrots and turmeric and cook for a further 3–4 minutes on a medium heat, stirring frequently.

Add the coconut milk, bring to the boil and simmer, covered, for 10 minutes or until the carrots are tender. Taste and adjust the seasoning, then serve hot, warm or cold.

COUSCOUS with roast tomatoes, peppers and goats' cheese

This is a distinctly modern, European way of using couscous, topped with an unctuous, deeply flavoured sauce made from roasted tomatoes and peppers and finished with chunks of roasted onion, pepper and tomatoes and salty goats' cheese. I cannot claim the idea as my own, sadly, since I stole it from a press release for an Italian product and then reworked it, to do without the poor product in question. Apologies to the public relations company and the producers and thanks for a great idea.

SERVES 4

8 PLUM TOMATOES, HALVED

1 RED ONION, QUARTERED

2 RED PEPPERS, SEEDED AND CUT INTO LARGE CHUNKS

1 FRESH RED CHILLI

4 GARLIC CLOVES

2 SPRIGS OF THYME

3 TABLESPOONS OLIVE OIL

1 TABLESPOON SHERRY VINEGAR

1 TABLESPOON CASTER SUGAR

SALT AND FRESHLY GROUND BLACK PEPPER

FOR THE COUSCOUS:

310 G (11 OZ) COUSCOUS

600 ML (1 PINT) HOT CHICKEN OR VEGETABLE STOCK

2 TABLESPOONS OLIVE OIL

3 TABLESPOONS CHOPPED PARSLEY

115 G (4 OZ) GOATS' CHEESE, DE-RINDED AND ROUGHLY DICED

6 BASIL LEAVES, SHREDDED

METHOD

Pre-heat the oven to 220°C/425°F/Gas Mark 7. Oil a large, shallow, ovenproof dish or roasting tin. Place the plum tomatoes in it in a single layer, cut-side up, along with the onion quarters, the peppers, the whole chilli and the garlic. Tuck the thyme sprigs amongst them. Drizzle over the olive oil and the sherry vinegar. Then sprinkle on the sugar, salt and pepper. Bake, uncovered, for 40–50 minutes, until the onions are beginning to brown at the edges.

Meanwhile, put the couscous into a bowl and pour on the steaming hot stock. Leave for 15 minutes, until all the liquid has been absorbed, stirring once or twice. Drizzle over the olive oil and mix well. Cover with foil and keep warm.

When the vegetables are done, pick out about half the tomatoes, peppers and onions and keep warm. Unless you want a hot sauce, remove the chilli. Tip the rest into a food processor, scraping in any juices and caramelized brown goo. Don't worry about the garlic skins. Process until smooth; then sieve. Thin with a little water or stock if necessary. Taste and adjust the seasoning.

Take the couscous out of the oven, add the parsley and fork up a little to mix in the greenery and separate the grains. Pile up in a serving dish. Pour over the sauce, arrange the reserved vegetables on top and scatter with goats' cheese and basil shreds. Serve hot.

fresh hyssop and cornmeal focaccia

Based on recipes for Italian focaccia, this bread takes on a golden yellow hue from the cornmeal in the dough and an aromatic warmth from the fresh hyssop. If you can't get fresh hyssop, use dried, about half the amount, either worked into the dough or sprinkled on top before the final rising and baking. The bread is brilliant with cheese (particularly goats' cheese or blue cheeses) and also makes lovely chunky sandwiches, split in two. If you have any left over, it toasts very nicely indeed.

MAKES A 30 x 20 CM (12 x 8 IN) FLAT LOAF

450 G (1 LB) STRONG WHITE FLOUR, PLUS EXTRA FOR KNEADING

500 ML (18 FL OZ) WARM WATER

7 G SACHET OF EASY-BLEND YEAST

2 TEASPOONS LIGHT MUSCOVADO SUGAR

250 G (9 OZ) CORNMEAL OR POLENTA

1 TABLESPOON SALT

6 TABLESPOONS OLIVE OIL, PLUS EXTRA TO FINISH

4 TABLESPOONS CHOPPED HYSSOP LEAVES

COARSE SEA SALT, TO SCATTER OVER THE DOUGH

METHOD

Sift one-third of the flour. Put the warm water into a large bowl and whisk in the sifted flour, the yeast and sugar. Keep whisking until smooth, then cover with a damp tea towel and leave in a warm place for at least 30 minutes and up to 2 hours.

Now mix in the remaining flour, the cornmeal and salt. Stir to make a wet dough. If you have a mixer with a bread hook, now is the time to get it out. If you don't, then prepare to get messy. With a mixer, scrape the dough into the bowl and add 3 tablespoons of the olive oil. Knead slowly, adding a little flour here and there, until the dough begins to stretch and develop elasticity – usually after about 5 minutes.

With no mixer to hand, leave the dough in the bowl and pour over 3 tablespoons of the olive oil. Oil your hands, then plunge them under the wet dough, scooping it up and stretching it damply, then turning it over and letting it fall back down. At first it will just be soggy lumps. but soon the gluten will start to develop and it will begin to stretch. Sprinkle the dough with a little flour as you knead to flesh it out, and keep going for about 5 minutes, turning and stretching the dough. When the dough feels smoother and elastic, cover again with a damp tea towel and leave in a warm place for about an hour, until doubled in bulk.

Come back to the dough, drizzle over the remaining olive oil and sprinkle over the hyssop. Repeat the same sort of kneading, again dusting lightly with flour as you go, for 5 minutes or so. Now tip the dough into an oiled 30 x 20 cm (12 x 8 in) baking tin and spread and tease it out to the corners with freshly oiled hands. Smear a little more oil over the top, then push your fingers down into the dough here and there to make nice dimples. Scatter with coarse salt, then leave to rise again for another hour or so, covered with a damp tea towel.

Pre-heat the oven to 220°C/425°F/Gas Mark 7. Bake the bread for 25–30 minutes, until golden brown and cooked through. Run a knife round the edge, then turn out on to a wire rack. For best eating, serve warm from the oven.

rice salad with apricots

This salad tastes wonderful if you start on it while the rice is still hot as it absorbs some of the dressing as it cools. Either way, it tastes good, and is just the thing for a summer lunch, barbecue or picnic.

SERVES 4

ABOUT 350 G (12 OZ) LONG-GRAIN RICE, COOKED AND DRAINED

1 SMALL ONION, FINELY CHOPPED

1 GARLIC CLOVE, FINELY CHOPPED

1 TABLESPOON SUNFLOWER OR OLIVE OIL

6 SPRING ONIONS, THINLY SLICED

85 G (3 OZ) READY-TO-EAT DRIED APRICOTS, FINELY DICED

2–3 TABLESPOONS CHOPPED CORIANDER

FOR THE DRESSING:

1½ TABLESPOONS WHITE WINE VINEGAR

½ TEASPOON DIJON MUSTARD

4 TABLESPOONS SUNFLOWER OR OLIVE OIL

PLENTY OF SALT AND FRESHLY GROUND BLACK PEPPER

METHOD

As soon as the rice is cooked, tip it into a sieve and rinse with hot water, then leave to drain again. Make the dressing while the rice is still hot by whisking the vinegar with the mustard, salt and pepper, then gradually whisking in the oil. Taste and adjust the seasoning, bearing in mind that it needs to be slightly sharper and saltier than usual to balance the blandness of the rice. Tip the rice and dressing into a bowl and mix, then leave to cool – refrigerate if leaving overnight.

To finish the salad, fry the onion and garlic gently in the oil until tender and translucent. Mix into the rice along with the remaining ingredients. Taste again and adjust the seasoning one final time before serving.

chorizo and egg bread

This is an impressive answer to the sausage roll (from the Extremadura region in Spain) – on a big scale, and with whole baked eggs thrown in, into the bargain. Bread is filled with a whole hoop of chorizo, and as it bakes, some of the fat seeps out into the dough, staining it flaming orange-red and flavouring it right through. It's best eaten on the day it is made, still warm from the oven, but it will keep for a day or so after.

SERVES 6-8

30 G (1 OZ) FRESH YEAST OR 15 G (½ OZ) DRIED YEAST

1 TEASPOON CASTER SUGAR

750 G (1 LB 10 OZ) STRONG WHITE FLOUR

½ TABLESPOON SALT

2 TABLESPOONS OLIVE OIL

1 HORSESHOE-SHAPED COOKING CHORIZO OR ABOUT 300-350 G (10-12 OZ)
   LINKED SMALL COOKING CHORIZOS

4 EGGS

METHOD

Cream the yeast and sugar with about 150 ml (¼ pint) warm water. Leave in a warm place for 10 minutes or so until frothing. Sift the flour with the salt, make a well in the centre and add the yeast mixture and olive oil. Gradually mix in another 150 ml (5 fl oz) warm water (you may need a little extra) to form a soft, slightly sticky dough. Knead vigorously for 10 minutes, then return to the bowl, dust lightly with flour and cover with a damp tea towel. Leave in a warm place for 1–1½ hours, until doubled in bulk. Punch down and knead again for 5 minutes, then divide in half.

On a floured board, roll out half the dough to form a large oval about 5 cm (2 in) bigger all the way round than the horseshoe of chorizo (or the links when laid in an oval shape). My dough measured roughly 30 x 25 cm (12 x 10 in). Place the dough on a floured baking tray. Snip any string or metal tags off the chorizos (but don't separate the links, or skin it) and lay it on the bread dough.

Roll out the remaining dough to form an oval of the same size as the first. Moisten the dough around and inside the chorizo with water. Lay the second oval of dough on top and press down firmly to seal all around the chorizo. Brush the central dip in the middle of the chorizo with a little more water and press the whole eggs, still in their shells, gently down into the dip so that they sit in a nice neat row. Leave in a warm place for a further 30 minutes or so.

Pre-heat the oven to 180°C/350°F/Gas Mark 4. Bake the bread in the oven for 35–40 minutes. Tap the underneath – if it sounds hollow, it is cooked. Cool on a wire rack.

6

sweet things

chocolate meringue cake with cherries and mascarpone ■ summer pudding ■ a summer's delight ■ frances bendixon's ultimate pumpkin pie ■ almond, ricotta and honey cheesecake ■ compote of apples and raisins with nutmeg and greek yoghurt ■ tarte aux pignons ■ seville orange curd ■ lemon mascarpone ice-cream with strawberry coulis ■ golden eve's pudding ■ strawberry and fresh angelica tart ■ grilled figs with orange, honey and pecan sauce ■ raspberry and almond tart ■ lemon grass and ginger lemonade

chocolate meringue cake
with cherries and mascarpone

It is a shame that Black Forest gateau has been so bastardized and ruined by commerce, since cherries and chocolate are a natural partnership. Raspberries, too, go blissfully well with chocolate. This chocolate cake, slathered with rich mascarpone and fruit, is even more indulgent than a proper Black Forest gateau. The cake is crisp and meringue-like on the outside and fudgy with chocolate on the inside. All in all, this makes an indecently rich and wicked pudding. For an even fudgier interior, but a slightly less crisp top, leave the cake to stand overnight covered with a clean tea towel. If you don't like mascarpone, just serve with whipped cream alone.

SERVES 8

115 G (4 OZ) PLAIN CHOCOLATE

115 G (4 OZ) UNSALTED BUTTER, SOFTENED

3 EGGS, SEPARATED

30 G (1 OZ) PLAIN FLOUR

115 G (4 OZ) CASTER SUGAR

TO SERVE:

150 ML (¼ PINT) WHIPPING CREAM, WHIPPED

225 G (8 OZ) MASCARPONE

450 G (1 LB) CHERRIES, STONED, OR RASPBERRIES

METHOD

Pre-heat the oven to 160°C/325°F/Gas Mark 3. Line the base of a 19–20 cm (7½–8 in) cake tin with a circle of non-stick baking parchment and butter the sides generously.

Break the chocolate into squares or chop it in a food processor, place in a bowl above a pan of simmering water and melt it. As soon as it has melted, take the bowl off the heat. Beat in half the butter, a little at a time, and then the egg yolks.

Blend the flour with the remaining butter until soft and evenly mixed and stir into the chocolate mixture until completely amalgamated. Whisk the egg whites until stiff, add half the sugar and whisk again, until shiny and thick. Fold in the remaining sugar. Lightly fold the meringue into the chocolate mixture and pour into the cake tin. Stand the tin in a roasting tin half-filled with hot water and bake for 1¼ hours. Remove from the oven and leave to cool. Turn out just before serving.

Fold the whipped cream into the mascarpone. Either pile high on the cake and top with a tumble of cherries or raspberries, or arrange slices of cake on individual plates, with a large dollop of mascarpone cream and a generous mound of fruit scattered over. Devour.

summer pudding

This has to be one of my all-time top-ten puddings. When the sun is shining, head off to that pick-your-own farm and get picking so that you can enjoy summer pudding made with the freshest, juiciest fruit imaginable. One small note – use a decent loaf of bread. Sliced white may be very convenient, but when soaked with juice it turns unpleasantly slimy – a horribly cruel demise for one of the great British puddings.

I like to use *crème de cassis*, the French blackcurrant liqueur, to add depth of flavour to the juices, but if you don't have any, try adding a splash of undiluted Ribena or other blackcurrant cordial. If you take your pudding on a picnic, don't forget to take a sturdy shallow plate as well to turn it out on – cardboard disposables won't do.

SERVES 4

750 G (1 LB 10 OZ) MIXED SUMMER FRUIT – RASPBERRIES, RED, WHITE AND
   BLACKCURRANTS, TAYBERRIES, LOGANBERRIES, BLACKBERRIES,
   CHERRIES, BLUEBERRIES, ETC.
140 G (5 OZ) CASTER SUGAR
2 TABLESPOONS *CRÈME DE CASSIS* OR RIBENA
1 MEDIUM LOAF OF GOOD-QUALITY WHITE BREAD, THINLY SLICED,
   CRUSTS REMOVED

METHOD

Mix the fruit with the sugar in a saucepan. If you have time, cover with a tea towel or clingfilm and leave for a few hours to get the juices running. Place the pan over the heat and bring gently up to the boil, then simmer for about 3 minutes. Draw off the heat and stir in the cassis or Ribena. Carefully spoon out about 2 tablespoons of juice and set aside in a small bowl.

Rinse a 1 litre (1¾ pint) bowl with cold water, then shake out the excess. Cut a round out of one piece of bread to fit the bottom of the bowl, then cut the remaining slices into more or less triangular wedges. Line the sides of the bowl with wedges of bread, nudging them tightly together so that there are no gaps. Spoon in all the fruit and their juices (apart from the reserved juice). Cover the surface with more wedges of bread. Find a saucer that fits neatly inside the bowl, place it on the upper layer of bread, then weight it down with weights, bags of rice, tins of baked beans, or whatever comes to hand. Leave in the fridge overnight.

Remove the weights and saucer, run a thin-bladed knife around the edges of the pudding, then invert it on to a shallow serving plate. Brush the reserved juice over any blotchy, whitish patches and then just pour the last few drops over the pudding to burnish it. Serve with cream.

a summer's delight

Meringue, cream, strawberries and roses – the very essence of an English summer. Folded together and piled up high, with a deep red coulis of roses drizzled over the sides, this is a show-stopping pudding.

For the ultimate delight, make the meringues yourself, but for a last-minute afterthought, cheat with high-quality bought ones.

SERVES 5-6

500 G (1 LB 2 OZ) RIPE STRAWBERRIES

60 G (2 OZ) VANILLA SUGAR

1 TABLESPOON ROSE WATER

300 ML (½ PINT) WHIPPING CREAM

60 G (2 OZ) MERINGUES, ROUGHLY CRUSHED

5-6 SPRIGS OF MINT

PETALS OF 1 FRAGRANT DARK RED
   OR DEEP PINK ROSE

FOR THE ROSE COULIS:

3 FRAGRANT DEEP PINK ROSES

60 G (2 OZ) CASTER SUGAR

2 TABLESPOONS ORANGE JUICE

2 TABLESPOONS LEMON JUICE

METHOD

Hull the strawberries and halve, or quarter if large. Mix in a bowl with the sugar and rosewater, then cover and leave for at least an hour and up to 4 hours, as long as the room is not too warm. In high summer, leave in the fridge so that they don't start to ferment!

To make the rose coulis, separate the rose petals, removing the white heels if you have the time and inclination, then liquidize with the sugar, orange juice and lemon juice until smooth.

Just before serving, whip the cream until it just holds its shape, then lightly fold in the strawberry mixture and the pieces of meringue. Pile into individual sundae glasses, drizzle over a little of the rose coulis, then decorate with a sprig of mint and 2 or 3 fresh rose petals.

Alternatively, pile into one large crystal bowl, drizzling rose coulis between dollops and letting the last of it trickle down the sides. Scatter with fresh rose petals and serve.

frances bendixon's
ultimate pumpkin pie

There are as many recipes for pumpkin pie (the essential American Thanksgiving dessert) as there are people who make it. Although Frances Bendixon's ancestors were among the pilgrims who set sail for New England on the Mayflower back in the 17th century, she makes no claims to cooking the authentic pumpkin pie. She cooks the ultimate pumpkin pie. The secret is to use double cream (rather than milk or evaporated milk) and, most importantly, to drain the pumpkin purée overnight. This pie is so rich that it really doesn't need any embellishment. However, if you insist on going right over the top, serve it with whipped cream flavoured with brandy, or a scoop of vanilla ice cream.

SERVES 6-8

280 G (10 OZ) SHORTCRUST PASTRY (SEE PAGE 141)

2 LARGE EGGS

400 G (14 OZ) THOROUGHLY DRAINED PUMPKIN OR SQUASH PURÉE

1½ TEASPOONS GROUND CINNAMON

½ TEASPOON GROUND GINGER

½ TEASPOON GROUND ALLSPICE

½ TEASPOON SALT

250 ML (9 FL OZ) DOUBLE CREAM

125 ML (4 FL OZ) MAPLE SYRUP, OR TO TASTE

METHOD

Place a baking sheet in the oven and heat to 220°C/425°F/Gas Mark 7. Line a deep 23 cm (9 in) pie plate or tart tin with the pastry. Use a fork to decorate the rim. Prick the base with a fork and chill until needed.

To prepare the pumpkin or squash purée: take a 1.25 kg (2 lb 12 oz) wedge of pumpkin or other winter squash, or three large butternut squashes. Cut in half if necessary, and remove the seeds and fibres in the centre. Place on an oiled baking sheet, cut sides down, cover with foil and bake at 190°C/375°F/Gas Mark 5 until soft – anything from 40 minutes to 2½ hours! Leave on the sheet until cool enough to handle. Scoop out the pulp and process until smooth. Tip into a colander lined with split-open coffee filters or a double layer of muslin and leave to drain overnight. This long draining, to eliminate any wateriness, makes all the difference between take-it-or-leave-it pumpkin pie, and a very more-ish one. (It's a trick worth remembering when making other recipes requiring pumpkin purée).

Next, beat the eggs, then beat in the pumpkin or squash purée, followed by the spices and salt, then the cream. Add the maple syrup gradually, tasting as you do so. If you use a sweet squash, you may not need all of it. Taste and add extra spices if you think it needs a little more pepping up. Pour the mixture into the pastry case.

Place the filled case on the hot baking sheet in the oven. Bake for

10 minutes to start the crust browning, then reduce the heat to 190°C/375°F/ Gas Mark 5. Cook for about 30 minutes or until the filling looks set around the edges and about halfway to the middle of the pie, but the centre is still a bit wobbly. Serve warm or cold.

almond, ricotta and honey
cheesecake

This is a recipe I've had for a long time, based on a baked cheesecake that I ate in a now-defunct restaurant in London. It brings together a quartet of ingredients – ricotta, almonds, lemon, honey – that seems quintessentially Sicilian. What makes this version special is that unblanched almonds are used – that is, almonds that are still in their velvety brown skins – so that the baked filling is flecked with brown and has a pure almond-laden flavour.

SERVES 6-8

300 G (10 OZ) SHORTCRUST PASTRY (SEE PAGE 141)

85 G (3 OZ) UNBLANCHED ALMONDS

450 G (1 LB) RICOTTA CHEESE

3 EGGS, SEPARATED

5 TABLESPOONS HONEY

3 TABLESPOONS CASTER SUGAR

A PINCH OF SALT

FINELY GRATED ZEST OF 1 LEMON

JUICE OF ½ LEMON

METHOD

Use the pastry to line a tart tin 5 cm (2 in) deep and about 23 cm (9 in) in diameter with a removable base. Crimp the edges. Rest in the fridge for 30 minutes.

Pre-heat the oven to 190°C/375°F/Gas Mark 5.

Prick the base of the pastry case, line with foil or greaseproof paper and fill with baking beans. Bake in the oven for 10 minutes. Remove the beans and foil, and return to the oven for 3–5 minutes to dry out. Cool until tepid or cold.

To make the filling, grind the unblanched almonds to a powder. Beat the ricotta until smooth, then beat in the egg yolks, honey, sugar, salt, lemon zest and juice, and the ground almonds. Whisk the egg whites stiffly and fold into the ricotta mixture. Spoon into the pastry case. Bake at 180°C/350°F/Gas Mark 4 for 30–40 minutes until just set. Leave to cool in the tin, then chill for 4 hours. Unmould and serve.

compote of apples and raisins
with nutmeg and greek yoghurt

This compote of apples and raisins is one that we make in copious quantities every year when the apples ripen in our garden. We eat it for pudding (the children love it) and for breakfast, and it can be used as a pie or tart filling as well, if the fancy takes you. It can be made several days in advance, and served warm or cold. The mild creamy tartness of Greek yoghurt balances the sweetness.

SERVES 4

115 G (4 OZ) CASTER SUGAR

85 G (3 OZ) LIGHT MUSCOVADO SUGAR

450 ML (16 FL OZ) WATER

500 G (1 LB 2 OZ) GOOD EATING APPLES (MORE OR LESS – DON'T
   WASTE HALF AN APPLE TO GET THE EXACT QUANTITY), PEELED,
   CORED AND CUT INTO EIGHTHS

60 G (2 OZ) RAISINS

FRESHLY GRATED NUTMEG

4 TABLESPOONS GREEK YOGHURT, TO SERVE

METHOD

Put the two sugars into a pan with the water and stir over a moderate heat until completely dissolved. Bring up to the boil. Add the apples and raisins, and a scraping of fresh nutmeg. Simmer very gently for about 30 minutes, until the apple slices are translucent and very tender. Scoop them out into a shallow dish or bowl with a slotted spoon and add another fresh rasping of nutmeg. Boil the juice down for 3 or 4 minutes, until syrupy, then pour it over the apples. Serve warm or cold with the Greek yoghurt.

tarte aux pignons

There are many versions of the Provençal pine nut tart, some made with shortcrust pastry, some filled with custard. This particular one has to be among the best. It is quite my favourite pine nut dessert, with a soft, gooey, scented filling, studded with browned pine nuts. It comes from an American book called *Cooking Provence* by Antoine Bouterin, a Provençal chef.

SERVES 6

250 G (9 OZ) PUFF PASTRY

FOR THE FILLING:

130 G (4½ OZ) GROUND ALMONDS

FINELY GRATED ZEST OF 1 ORANGE

225 G (8 OZ) CASTER SUGAR

1 TABLESPOON ORANGE-FLOWER WATER

2 TABLESPOONS HONEY

2 LARGE EGGS, BEATEN

2 TABLESPOONS EXTRA VIRGIN OLIVE OIL

115 G (4 OZ) PINE NUTS

METHOD

Pre-heat the oven to 200°C/400°F/Gas Mark 6.

Roll the pastry out very thinly and use it to line a 20–23 cm (8–9 in) tart tin, doubling the pastry over the rim to make a double-thickness rim, and crimping it securely. Prick the base with a fork and leave it to rest for 30 minutes in the fridge. Cover the pastry base with a square of buttered cooking foil (butter-side down!), fill the case with baking beans and bake blind for about 10 minutes. Remove the beans and foil and return the pastry case to the oven for about another 10 minutes to dry out, without colouring. Leave to cool.

To make the filling, put the ground almonds in a bowl and add the orange zest and sugar. Mix, make a well in the centre and then add the orange-flower water, honey, eggs and oil. Mix thoroughly to give a thick, smooth batter. Tip in two-thirds of the pine nuts, pour the mixture into the pastry case and sprinkle evenly with the remaining pine nuts. Bake until browned and almost, but not quite, firm in the centre: about 20–25 minutes.

seville orange curd

If you've never tasted home-made lemon curd, then you have missed out on one of the most delicious preserves in the world. This Seville orange curd is very special too, with the bitter tartness of the juice softened and tamed by the butter, sugar and eggs. Anyone who likes marmalade is bound to love it, and those who are not so keen on marmalade, like myself, take to it with alacrity, too.

If you want to make straight lemon curd, just substitute lemon juice and zest for the Seville juice and zest. Lime curd is fantastic too, but since limes are smaller than lemons but just as costly, it works out rather more expensive. Seville, lemon and lime curds do not have the longevity of jams and jellies. Once cooled, store in the fridge for up to four weeks. If you plan to give it to anyone as a present, mark a use-by date on the label.

MAKES AROUND 1.3 KG (2½ LB)

9–12 SEVILLE ORANGES

550 G (1 LB 4 OZ) CASTER SUGAR

225 G (8 OZ) UNSALTED BUTTER, DICED

5 LARGE EGGS

METHOD

One at a time, grate the zest of the Sevilles finely, then squeeze the juice and strain it into a measuring jug until you have 300 ml (½ pint). Pour into a bowl and add the zest, sugar and butter. Place the bowl over a pan of gently simmering water, making sure that the base of the bowl does not come into contact with the water. Stir until the butter is melted and the sugar has dissolved.

Beat the eggs lightly to loosen them, then strain through a sieve into the warm Seville orange and butter mixture. Stir constantly, over the gently simmering water, until the mixture has thickened enough to coat the back of a spoon – allow a good 20–25 minutes, but take great care not to let the curds get anywhere near boiling point. Woe betide you if you let your attention wander for more than a few seconds, for overheated curds will curdle and scramble to an unsightly and ruined mess. Actually, this rarely happens in my experience (never, so far, though I guess there is always a first time…) but remember my dire warnings nonetheless.

As soon as the mixture has thickened, lift the bowl out of the pan and pour the curd into warm, sterilized jars (see page 6). Seal tightly, label and leave to cool. Keep the curd in the fridge.

lemon mascarpone
ice-cream with strawberry coulis

This is inspired by a Venetian speciality called a *sgroppino*, which hovers halfway between a pudding and a cocktail. A true *sgroppino* is a blend of lemon ice-cream, strawberry purée and the Venetian dry sparkling wine, *prosecco*, all whisked together to a marvellous slush. To keep the cost down, I've ommited the *prosecco*, but this lemon and mascarpone ice-cream is just superb with its own strawberry coulis merely spooned over the top.

SERVES 2

45 G (1½ OZ) CASTER SUGAR

FINELY GRATED ZEST AND JUICE OF 1 LARGE LEMON
  (ABOUT 60 ML/2 FL OZ JUICE)

185 G (6½ OZ) MASCARPONE

FOR THE COULIS:

140 G (5 OZ) STRAWBERRIES, HULLED

10–20 G (⅓–⅔ OZ) ICING SUGAR

A DASH OF LEMON JUICE

METHOD

To make the ice-cream, put the sugar, half the lemon zest and 5 tablespoons of water into a pan. Stir over a moderate heat until the sugar has dissolved, then bring up to the boil and simmer for 2 minutes to make a syrup. Leave to cool.

Beat the lemon juice gradually into the mascarpone, adding the sugar syrup a little at a time until the mixture tastes just a touch on the sweet side (freezing always dulls the sweetness). Beat in the last of the lemon zest. If you have an ice-cream maker, freeze the mixture in that. If not, pour into a shallow container, cover and place in the freezer, turned to its lowest setting. When the sides have set (in my small freezer this takes around 1 hour), take the ice-cream out of the freezer, break up the frozen bits and push them towards the centre. Return to the freezer and repeat once more. Now leave the ice-cream until it is just about set solid but not yet rock-hard. Either scrape it into a food processor and process to a smooth mush to break up large ice crystals or tip it into a bowl and beat with all your might. As soon as it is done, pour it back into the container and return it to the freezer. If you can be bothered, it is no bad thing to go through this last process one more time for an even smoother ice-cream, but you can get away without.

To make the strawberry coulis, process the strawberries with the icing sugar (to taste) and the lemon juice. Cover and chill until needed. About 30 minutes before serving, transfer the ice-cream to the fridge to soften slightly.

To serve, divide the ice-cream between 2 beautiful stemmed glasses or sundae cups and then spoon over the strawberry coulis. Sheer, cooling, summertime bliss.

golden eve's pudding

Eve's pudding is one of those comforting, old-fashioned, utterly delicious autumn puddings, with a layer of soft apple at the bottom and a light sponge baked over the top. Well, this version hangs on to all that is good about the original but brings it bang up-to-date by replacing some of the flour with sunshine-yellow polenta (use the quick-cooking sort that most good supermarkets and Italian delis sell) and adding a clean dash of lemon. The polenta gives the topping a slightly grainy texture and a glossy golden crumb which is wonderfully appealing against the tender apple. An ideal pudding for any family lunch or supper.

If you make the apple base in advance, be sure to heat it up thoroughly before pouring it into the dish and covering with the polenta topping. You need that burst of heat from underneath to cook the golden sponge properly. If you pour it on to cold apple, you'll end up with a well-browned top and a runny batter underneath.

SERVES 4

675 G (1 LB 8 OZ) COOKING APPLES, PEELED, CORED AND CHOPPED

1 TABLESPOON HONEY

FINELY GRATED ZEST OF ½ LEMON

30 G (1 OZ) CASTER SUGAR

FOR THE TOPPING:

60 G (2 OZ) POLENTA

30 G (1 OZ) PLAIN FLOUR

1 TEASPOON BAKING POWDER

60 G (2 OZ) CASTER SUGAR

A PINCH OF SALT

FINELY GRATED ZEST OF ½ LEMON

1 EGG, LIGHTLY BEATEN

60 G (2 OZ) MELTED BUTTER, COOLED UNTIL TEPID

JUICE OF ½ LEMON

A LITTLE MILK (1–2 TABLESPOONS)

METHOD

Pre-heat the oven to 200°C/400°F/Gas Mark 6.

Put the apples into a pan with the honey, lemon zest and sugar. Cover and cook over a medium heat until the juice has begun to run – a mere 3–5 minutes should do it. Uncover and continue cooking until a fair proportion of the apples has collapsed to a purée but a few chunks remain intact (a further 10–15 minutes). Stir well, then tip into a 1.5 litre (2½ pint) pie dish and spread out.

To make the topping, mix all the dry ingredients, including the lemon zest, together in a bowl and make a well in the centre. Pour in the egg, melted butter and lemon juice and mix well, gradually bringing in the other ingredients. Add enough milk to give a loose dropping consistency. Dollop the mixture over the cooked apples, then carefully spread it out smoothly and evenly to cover them.

Bake for about 25–30 minutes, until the topping is firm to the touch and pulling away from the edges of the dish. Serve hot or warm, with single or double cream.

strawberry and fresh angelica tart

By infusing the angelica in the milk for the *crème pâtissière*, the classic French strawberry tart is elevated into one of the most sublime desserts. Make it for a party, for your loved ones or just for the pleasure of eating it yourself.

If you can only find those awful enormous watery apologies for strawberries that seem to have taken over these days, then you will do better to replace them with raspberries, or even tiny alpine strawberries, though they will set you back a pretty penny.

SERVES 8

ABOUT 1 KG (2 LB 4 OZ) SMALL STRAWBERRIES
ICING SUGAR, FOR DUSTING
ANGELICA LEAVES, TO GARNISH

FOR THE PÂTÉ SABLÉE:
300 G (10 OZ) PLAIN FLOUR
A PINCH OF SALT
100 G (3½ OZ) ICING SUGAR
200 G (7 OZ) UNSALTED BUTTER
2 EGG YOLKS

FOR THE CRÈME PÂTISSIÈRE:
350 ML (12 FL OZ) MILK
1 VANILLA POD
3 OR 4 (DEPENDING ON THICKNESS) 7.5 CM (1 IN) LENGTHS
  OF FRESH ANGELICA STEMS
A PINCH OF SALT
2 EGG YOLKS
60 G (2 OZ) CASTER SUGAR
45 G (1½ OZ) PLAIN FLOUR

METHOD

Both the *pâté sablée* and *crème pâtissière* should be made in advance. For the pastry, sift the flour with the salt and icing sugar. Process with the butter and egg yolks to form a soft dough. Scrape up into a ball. Knead briefly to smooth out, then wrap in clingfilm and chill for at least 4 hours.

Pre-heat the oven to 180°C/350°F/Gas Mark 4. Roll out the pastry and use to line a 25 cm (10 in) tart tin, gently easing it in – it will probably tear, but don't worry; just patch it up with the trimmings. Cover and chill for an hour. Prick the base with a fork. Line with greaseproof paper and weight down with baking beans. Bake blind for 20 minutes, then remove the beans and paper and return the pastry to the oven for another 15–20 minutes, until lightly browned and crisp. Cool on a wire rack.

To make the *crème pâtissière*, put the milk into a pan with the vanilla, angelica and salt. Bring gently to the boil, then turn down the heat very low, cover and leave for 30 minutes. (If you can't get a really low flame, just take the pan off the heat and set aside.) Whisk the egg yolks with the sugar until pale, then whisk in the flour. Gradually pour in the hot milk, whisking constantly. Pick out the angelica stems and the vanilla and discard. Return the milk mixture to the pan and bring slowly to the boil, whisking to smooth out as many lumps as possible. Let it bubble for 1 minute, keeping the heat low and stirring to prevent catching. Draw off the heat and leave until tepid. If not using immediately, rub a knob of butter over the surface to prevent a skin forming. Reheat gently before using, so it spreads easily.

As near as possible to serving, spread the *crème pâtissière* in the pastry case. Hull the strawberries and halve them. Arrange them in concentric circles, covering the *crème pâtissière*. Dust with a little icing sugar and garnish with angelica leaves.

grilled figs with orange, honey and pecan sauce

This is a pretty, light pudding for early autumn, when purple or green figs are at their plumpest and most succulent. Blanch the zest and prepare the sauce in advance; then there is precious little to do when it comes to finishing the pudding for serving.

SERVES 4

1 ORANGE

2 TABLESPOONS OF HONEY

60 G (2 OZ) BUTTER

1 TABLESPOON OF ICING SUGAR

5 CM (2 IN) SPRIG OF ROSEMARY

8 FIGS, HALVED

60 G (2 OZ) SHELLED PECANS

SINGLE CREAM, TO SERVE

METHOD

Pare the zest from the orange and cut it into fine shreds (or use a zester). Blanch the shreds in boiling water for a minute, drain and repeat. Reserve. Squeeze the juice from the orange and place it in a pan with the honey, butter, icing sugar and rosemary. Stir over a low heat for 5 minutes, until smoothly mixed. Set aside until needed.

Shortly before you wish to serve, pre-heat the grill thoroughly. Brush the cut sides of the figs with a little of the sauce and grill until sizzling and lightly browned. Meanwhile, remove the rosemary sprig from the sauce, add the pecans and re-heat. Arrange the figs on individual plates, spoon some of the sauce around them and garnish with the blanched orange zest. Serve immediately, with single cream.

raspberry and almond tart

In essence this is a glorified form of almond shortbread, rolled out thickly to line a tart tin. A thin layer of raspberry jam covers it, topped with a lattice of pastry. The quality of the jam will regulate the quality of the final tart. Home-made is best, but otherwise a really good bought one, made with a high proportion of fruit to sugar, is essential.

Since the dough is very rich, it can be a little tricky to handle. Don't worry. Press the dough into the tin, and use your fingers to smooth over any tears or holes. Lay the dough strips over the jam using a palette knife. If the odd one breaks as you lay it down, just pinch the ends together: as a whole tart is dusted with icing sugar before serving, it won't show too much.

SERVES 6-8

150 G (5 OZ) FLOUR

½ TEASPOON OF GROUND CINNAMON

PINCH OF SALT

140 G (5 OZ) CASTER SUGAR

140 G (5 OZ) GROUND ALMONDS

ZEST OF 1 LEMON, FINELY GRATED

140 G (5 OZ) BUTTER, SOFTENED

2 EGG YOLKS

200 G (7 OZ) BEST-QUALITY RASPBERRY JAM

ICING SUGAR

METHOD

Sift the flour with the cinnamon and salt. Mix with the sugar, ground almonds and lemon zest. Make a well in the centre and place the butter and egg yolks in it. Using a palette knife at first, and then the tips of your fingers, work to a dough. Knead briefly to smooth out. Break off about a quarter of the pastry and wrap in cling film. Wrap the larger part in cling film, then chill both for 30 minutes.

Roll out the larger ball of pastry (leave the rest in the fridge for the moment) to a thickness of 5 mm (¼ in) and line a 24 cm (9½ in) buttered and floured tart tin with it. Prick with a fork and spread evenly with the jam. Roll out the remaining pastry and trimmings and cut into long strips 1 cm (½ in) wide. Use these to make a lattice pattern over the jam, pressing the ends on to the edge of the pastry case. Rest for 30 minutes in the fridge.

Place a baking tray in the oven, and pre-heat to 200°C/400°F/Gas Mark 6. Set the tart on the hot baking tray and cook for 25–30 minutes, until nicely browned. Cool and dust lightly with icing sugar before serving.

lemon grass and ginger lemonade

Home-made lemonade, served in a glass beaded with icy condensation, is blissfully refreshing on a hot summer's day. There are lots of variations on the theme, but I particularly like this one, with the scent of lemon grass and the ticklish hint of ginger.

SERVES 4-6

4 LEMON GRASS STEMS, BRUISED HEAVILY AND FINELY SLICED

20 G (¾ OZ) FRESH ROOT GINGER, CHOPPED

115 G (4 OZ) CASTER SUGAR

200 ML (7 FL OZ) WATER

JUICE OF 2 LEMONS

600–850 ML (1–1½ PINTS) SPARKLING MINERAL WATER

ICE CUBES, A FEW SLICES OF LEMON, A FEW SPRIGS OF MINT,
    AND A FEW BORAGE FLOWERS, IF AVAILABLE, TO SERVE

METHOD

Put the lemon grass, ginger, sugar and water in a saucepan and stir over a moderate heat until the sugar has dissolved. Bring up to the boil and simmer for 10 minutes. Leave to cool, then strain.

Mix the syrup with the lemon juice and mineral water to taste. Serve in tall glasses with plenty of ice, and a slice of lemon, a sprig of mint and a couple of borage flowers, if you have them, afloat in each one.

basic recipes

tomato sauce

I offer you three alternatives here, all of them turning out a very good, relatively smooth tomato sauce, with allowances for the lesser quality of North European tomatoes. Tomato purée and a little sugar compensate to some degree, and so too does generous seasoning.

The first is the kind of sauce to make in high summer, when fresh tomatoes are at their cheapest, ripest and sweetest. At other times of the year passata (sieved tomato purée) is a perfectly acceptable alternative. In Sicily most households make enough passata to see them through the winter, crammed into wine bottles and sterilized so it will keep. The passata or 'creamed tomatoes' that is sold here in bottles or cartons in most supermarkets is pretty good.

The other tomato preserve made all over the island is estratto, an immensely thick and salty, semi-dried tomato paste. The concentrated caramelized flavour adds a marvellous depth to sauces. The nearest I can get to it is by using a mixture of sun-dried tomato and tomato purée.

with fresh tomatoes

MAKES ABOUT 600 ML (1 PINT)

900 G (1 LB) RIPE TOMATOES, SKINNED AND
    SEEDED
1 LARGE ONION, CHOPPED
3 GARLIC CLOVES, CHOPPED
3 TABLESPOONS OLIVE OIL
2 TABLESPOONS TOMATO PURÉE
½–1 TABLESPOON SUGAR
SALT AND FRESHLY GROUND BLACK PEPPER
3 SPRIGS OF BASIL

Liquidize or process the tomatoes. Place the onion, garlic and olive oil in a large pan and cook over a medium heat until the onion is tender. Add the processed tomatoes, tomato purée, sugar, salt and pepper and simmer gently for 30 minutes. Now add the basil and cook for a further 5–10 minutes. Taste and add a little more sugar if the sauce is on the sharp side. Adjust the seasoning. Before using, make sure you remove the sprigs of basil.

with passata

Make as before, substituting 600 ml (1 pint) passata for the processed tomatoes.

with estratto (or as near as you can get)

Make as before. Use the same quantity of fresh tomatoes or passata, but make the tomato purée as follows: process 4 tablespoons tomato purée with 60 g (2 oz) roughly chopped sun-dried tomatoes that have been preserved in olive oil and add to the sauce along with the tomatoes.

shortcrust pastry

MAKES 350 G (12 OZ) SHORTCRUST PASTRY

225 G (8 OZ) PLAIN FLOUR
PINCH OF SALT
115 G (4 OZ) CHILLED BUTTER, DICED
1 EGG YOLK, BEATEN
ICED WATER

Sift the flour with the salt. Rub the butter into the flour until it resembles fine breadcrumbs. Make a well in the centre and add the egg yolk and enough iced water to form a soft dough – 1½-2 tablespoons of water should be enough. Mix quickly and lightly, and knead very briefly to smooth out. Wrap and chill for at least 30 minutes in the fridge. Bring the pastry back to room temperature before using.

basic vinaigrette

Please don't waste your money on bottles of ready-made French dressing. They are ridiculously expensive and not terribly good either. Making a proper vinaigrette or French dressing is child's play. Of course, you'll have to invest in a decent bottle of oil or plainer groundnut oil, and another of wine vinegar, but they can be used for other things too.

Any left-over vinaigrette will keep in a screw-top jar in the fridge for several weeks. In fact, I usually make double or treble quantities, so that there's plenty left to use at a moment's notice.

ENOUGH FOR A GENEROUS 6 PERSON SALAD

1 TABLESPOON WHITE WINE VINEGAR

4-5 TABLESPOONS OLIVE OIL OR GROUNDNUT OIL

½ TEASPOON DIJON MUSTARD (OPTIONAL)

SALT AND FRESHLY GROUND BLACK PEPPER

Mix the vinegar with the mustard, salt and pepper in a bowl. Whisk in the oil, a tablespoon at a time. After the fourth spoonful, taste – if it is on the sharp side, whisk in the last spoonful of oil and more if necessary. Adjust seasonings.

Alternatively put all ingredients into a screw-top jar, close tightly and shake to mix. Taste and adjust seasoning or add more oil, as necessary.

tapenade

Dark, pungent tapenade is one of the defining flourishes of Provençal food. A blend of black olives, capers (tapena is the Provençal word for capers), anchovies and a variable collection of other background elements, including, sometimes, tuna fish, it turns up here, there and everywhere – except in sweet dishes, naturally.

The making of tapenade is easy; what is more testing is choosing the right olives. Chew on one before you buy, to make quite certain that you really like its taste. Don't buy them in a jar or tin, unless you know that you like the taste of that brand, and, above all, don't buy tinned stoned black olives, which, more often than not, taste soapy – something which will be sorrowfully emphasized in the tapenade. When the perfect small Niçoise olive is not on the cards, I find that the big juicy Greek Kalamatas make a good tapenade.

SERVES 8-10

250 G (9 OZ) BLACK OLIVES, STONED

4 TINNED ANCHOVY FILLETS

5 TABLESPOONS CAPERS, RINSED

2 GARLIC CLOVES, CHOPPED

2 TABLESPOONS LEMON JUICE

1 LEVEL TEASPOON FRESH THYME LEAVES

85 G (3 OZ) TINNED TUNA FISH (OPTIONAL)

½ TEASPOON FRESHLY GROUND BLACK PEPPER

75-100 ML (3-4 FL OZ) EXTRA VIRGIN OIL

To make the tapenade, put all the ingredients except the oil in the processor and process in brief bursts to give a slightly knobbly purée. Scrape out into a bowl and beat in the oil. If you are not using it immediately, cover with cling film and store in the fridge, where it will keep for a week or more.

index